Religious Education

ALSO AVAILABLE IN THE KEY DEBATES IN EDUCATIONAL POLICY SERIES

ALSO AVAILABLE FROM BLOOMSBURY

Religious Education

Educating for Diversity

L. PHILIP BARNES AND ANDREW DAVIS EDITED BY J. MARK HALSTEAD

Bloomsbury Academic
An imprint of Bloomsbury Publishing Plc

B L O O M S B U R Y

LONDON · NEW DELHI · NEW YORK · SYDNEY

Bloomsbury Academic
An imprint of Bloomsbury Publishing Plc

50 Bedford Square	1385 Broadway
London	New York
WC1B 3DP	NY 10018
UK	USA

www.bloomsbury.com

BLOOMSBURY and the Diana logo are trademarks of Bloomsbury Publishing Plc

First published 2015

British Library Cataloguing-in-Publication Data
A catalogue record for this book is available from the British Library.

ISBN: PB: 978-1-4725-7106-9
ePDF: 978-1-4725-7108-3
ePub: 978-1-4725-7107-6

Library of Congress Cataloging-in-Publication Data
A catalog record for this book is available from the Library of Congress.

Series: Key Debates in Educational Policy

Typeset by Integra Software Services Pvt. Ltd.
Printed and bound in India

Contents

Series Editor's Preface – Key Debates in Educational Policy

Christopher Winch

Impact pamphlets were launched in 1999 as an initiative of the Philosophy of Education Society of Great Britain. Their aim was to bring philosophical perspectives to bear on UK education policy and they have been written by leading general philosophers or philosophers of education. There are now more than twenty volumes.

They dealt with a variety of issues relating to policy within the field of education. Some have focused on controversial aspects of current government policy such as those by Andrew Davis on assessment, Harry Brighouse on disparities in secondary education, Mary Warnock on changes in provision for pupils with special educational needs, and Colin Richards on school inspection. Others, such as those by Michael Luntley on performance related pay and by Chris Winch on vocational education and training, have been critical of new policy initiatives. Yet others have been concerned with the organization and content of the school curriculum. These have included pamphlets by Kevin Williams on the teaching of foreign languages, Steve Bramall and John White on Curriculum 2000, David Archard on sex education, Stephen Johnson on thinking skills, Graham Haydon on Personal, Social and Health Education and John Gingell on the Visual Arts.

The launch of each pamphlet was been accompanied by a symposium for policy makers and others at which issues raised in the pamphlets have been further explored. These have been attended by government ministers, opposition spokespersons, other MPs, representatives from the Qualifications and Curriculum Authority, employers' organizations, trades unions and teachers' professional organizations as well as members of think tanks, academics and journalists.

Some of the original pamphlets have made a lasting impression on the world of education policy and have, in addition, sparked debates in both the policy and academic worlds. They have revealed a hunger for dealing with certain topics in a philosophically oriented way because it has been felt that the original pamphlet initiated a debate that needs and deserves to be taken a lot further. The Key Debates in Educational Policy series aimed to take some of these debates further by selecting from those original Impact pamphlets whose influence continues to be keenly felt and either reproducing or expanding them to take account of the most recent developments in the area with which they deal. In addition, each of the original pamphlets receives a lengthy reply by a distinguished figure in the area who takes issue with the main arguments of the original pamphlet. Each of the Key Debates volumes also contained a substantial foreword and/or afterword by an academic with strong interests in the area under discussion, which gave the context and provided extensive commentary on the questions under discussion and the arguments of the original author and his/her respondent.

There are a number of reasons for this. Philosophical techniques applied to policy issues can be very powerful tool clarifying questions and developing arguments based on ethical, aesthetic, political and epistemological positions. Philosophical argumentation is, however, by its nature, controversial and contested. There is rarely, if ever, one side to a philosophical question. The fact that the Impact pamphlets have often aroused lively debate and controversy is testament to this. There has been a hunger for a more rounded version of the debate to be presented in a format accessible to those who do not have a formal philosophical background but who find philosophical argumentation about educational issues to be useful in developing their own ideas. This series aimed to cater for this audience while also presenting rigorous argumentation that can also appeal to a more specialist audience.

It was hoped that each volume in this series would provide an introduction and set the scene to each topic and give the readership a splendid example of philosophical argumentation over a complex and important educational issue.

Notes on Contributors

L. Philip Barnes is Emeritus Reader in Religious and Theological Education at King's College London, UK. He has published widely in the field of religious education and is editor of a number of standard teacher education texts, including *Learning to Teach Religious Education in the Secondary School* (2008) and *Debates in Religious Education* (2012). His most recent book, entitled *Education, Religion and Diversity: Developing a New Model of Religious Education* (2014), both criticizes current theory and practice in religious education and develops the case for a new 'post-liberal' model of religious education.

Andrew Davis was a primary teacher for many years before lecturing at Cambridge and Durham Universities. He is currently an Honorary Research Fellow at Durham. He trained as an analytical philosopher specializing in philosophy of religion with Richard Swinburne. His publications include *The Limits of Educational Assessment* (1998) and co-authorship of the best-selling *Mathematical Knowledge for Primary Teachers* (Fourth Edition 2010, with Suggate and Goulding). He has recently returned to religious topics with 'Flawed Objections to Religious Pluralism: The Implications for Religious Education' *Philosophy of Education Society Yearbook* and 'Defending Religious Pluralism for Religious Education' *Ethics and Education*, both published in 2010. His short book *To Read or Not to Read: Decoding Synthetic Phonics* attracted widespread media attention in 2014.

J. Mark Halstead is Emeritus Professor of Education at the University of Huddersfield. He has written widely in the fields of moral education, multicultural education, Islamic education and the philosophy of education.

Acknowledgement

The contribution of Philip Barnes draws on his earlier, shorter discussion of some of the same issues in *Religious Education: Taking Religious Difference Seriously*, which was No 17 in the Philosophy of Education Society of Great Britain Impact series of policy discussions; some material is also taken from 'Relativism, Ineffability and the Appeal to Experience: A Reply to the Myth Makers', *Modern Theology* 7(1): 101–114.

Introduction

J. Mark Halstead

How to accommodate religious diversity in schools and other institutions is one of the most challenging and controversial issues facing educators today, and as such raises a plethora of questions. Should the state adopt a position of strict neutrality between different religious faiths and between belief and non-belief? What messages about religion do children pick up from such a stance? Should children be taught that all major world religions are simply different routes to the same spiritual goal and therefore in a sense all equally true? Where does this leave the belief within many religions that they have certain exclusive claims to truth that other faiths lack? What contribution can religious education make in society at large towards developing increased respect, tolerance and understanding towards different faiths and their adherents? What sort of philosophical and religious assumptions underpin this contribution? Is religion itself part of the problem in relation to intolerance, extremism and conflict in the world or part of the solution?

This book takes the form of a debate about the issues raised by these questions between two leading scholars in the field. The debate focuses on the kind of religious education that should be provided in modern liberal democratic states characterized by diversity, in the light of the philosophical and theological tensions that exist between religious exclusivism and religious pluralism. The purpose of the Introduction is to contextualize the debate in the policies of one particular country – the UK (and sometimes, more specifically, England) – though it is clear that since the book is broadly philosophical in its approach, there will be many resonances with other Western societies that share the same framework of liberal values.

The starting points for the debate, on which both authors agree, are the reality of religious diversity in contemporary societies, the belief that religious education should take religious differences seriously and the belief in the fair and equal treatment of different groups unless there are good grounds for treating them differently. Clearly, diversity, even religious diversity, takes many forms; for example, religions can be distinguished on the basis of whether they are proselytizing or non-proselytizing, exclusivist or pluralist, 'propositional' or 'experiential-expressivist' (to use Lindbeck's terminology: 1984, p. 34). For official purposes, however, the most significant form of religious diversity – perhaps because it is linked to people's core identity – is the existence of different world religions and denominations within a single country. It is this form of religious diversity which is highlighted by the one question on religious affiliation in the National Census for England and Wales in 2011: 'What is your religion?' Table 1, which compares the figures for 2001 (the first time the question about religious affiliation was asked) and the figures for 2011, identifies significant growth in religious diversity of this kind.

Table 1 Religious affiliation in England

Religion	Number in 2011	Percentage	Number in 2001	Percentage
Buddhist	238,626	0.5	139,046	0.3
Christian	31,479,876	59.4	35,251,244	71.7
Hindu	806,199	1.5	546,982	1.1
Jewish	261,282	0.5	257,671	0.5
Muslim	2,660,116	5.0	1,542,887	3.1
Sikh	420,196	0.8	327,343	0.7
Other	227,825	0.4	143,811	0.3
No religion	13,114,232	24.7	7,171,332	14.6
Not stated	3,804,104	7.2	3,776,515	7.7

Statistics taken from the Census for England and Wales: ONS (2013)

There are many complexities hidden within the census figures, however: first, they are based on self-identification, and membership of a religion may be difficult to define; second, the question is a voluntary one, and a significant percentage of the population chose not to respond; third, no distinction is made between practising and non-practising members of a faith; fourth, dividing people in a country up on the basis of major world faiths may obscure very serious divisions and potential conflicts *within* each faith, and the tendency of denominations to define themselves in terms of difference from other groups clearly contributes to a climate supportive of the kind of exclusivism which Davis criticizes so strongly. Nevertheless, the numbers provide a useful starting point not only for the implementation of anti-discrimination legislation but also for the prediction of future demographic trends relating to religious diversity. For example, the growth in the proportion of Muslims from 3 per cent to nearly 5 per cent of the total population of England and Wales over a 10-year period is already the biggest growth of any religious group, but the fact that over 9.1 per cent of the under-5 age group belong to Muslim families is a strong indicator that the proportion of Muslims is set to increase further (ONS, 2013).

In public policy, responses to the growing religious diversity in the UK are still based largely on liberal values: religion is seen as a private individual matter, and the freedom of individuals to follow their own faith and bring up their children in its precepts (so long as no harm to others is incurred by the exercise of such freedom) is guaranteed by human rights conventions as ratified by the British Parliament and built into the legal system. In spite of the special status of the Church of England, all faiths are treated with equal respect as far as practicable in order to avoid accusations of partiality or unfair treatment. Equality of respect may sometimes require differentiated treatment if the principle of avoiding putting minority faiths into a position where they are expected or required to act against their own religious beliefs and values is to be upheld. Thus turban-wearing Sikhs are exempt from British legislation relating to the wearing of head protection while riding motor-cycles or working on construction sites, and Muslims can generally expect to be provided with *halal* food in public institutions like schools and hospitals. Many of the multicultural policies that have been adopted over the last 40 years involve recognition of the specific religious beliefs and practices of religious minorities.

The response of individual citizens to religious diversity, on the other hand, has not always been so positive. Prejudice and discrimination abound, especially against Muslims, often fed by stories in the popular media, though it is not always easy to distinguish religious discrimination from racism. Numerous books and reports have tracked the growth of Islamophobia in recent years (Allen, 2010; Esposito and Kalin, 2011). The aftermath of 9/11 has combined with other factors in the new millennium to generate increased suspicion of Muslim and other fundamentalist groups, and multicultural education has been increasingly criticized for providing a context in which religious extremism could flourish. By 2007, politicians were regularly speaking of the 'death' of multiculturalism (Halstead, 2010), and new policies, less friendly to Muslims and other minorities, were developed with two main purposes: first, to counter terrorism and prevent extremism and second, to promote community cohesion and to encourage minorities to accept 'shared British values', defined in liberal terms as including freedom, tolerance, equality, human rights and respect for persons. As Husband and Alam (2011) point out, from a Muslim perspective there is a significant tension between these two policies.

Current government policy uses the language of 'the Big Society' in preference to that of 'community cohesion' but continues to balance intolerance of extremism with a continuing emphasis on 'shared British values' and a common understanding of the obligations of citizenship (Parker-Jenkins et al. 2014, pp. 23; 45–46). These values generally continue to underpin educational policy relating to religious diversity. Three main approaches are apparent. The first involves the creation of a school climate that makes at least some concessions to religious diversity. This typically includes making adaptations to institutional practices (such as school uniform, assemblies, respecting holy days, providing a prayer room, etc.) and minimally to the school curriculum (e.g. respecting religious sensitivities in areas like sex education). The second is to prepare all students for life in a culturally diverse society, particularly by encouraging tolerance, understanding and respect for difference. The third is to prevent religious extremism and support for terrorism by emphasizing common values and 'Britishness'. These values are in evidence across the curriculum but mainly in citizenship education, introduced as a National Curriculum subject in 2002, and Personal, Social and Health Education (PSHE).

The relationship between religious education and religious diversity, especially in state-funded schools, is more complex than it first appears. This may be because the subject's aims and content are partly determined politically, partly on educational grounds and partly in accordance with the distinctive concepts and truth criteria of the subject matter. If they were purely a political matter, decisions about the subject could be much more straightforward. Religious education would be designed to contribute to the development of responsible and respectful relationships between people from different faith backgrounds. It would be about challenging religious prejudice and intolerance by increasing children's knowledge and understanding of the diverse beliefs, values and practices of different faiths and worldviews. Each faith would be treated with equal respect and would be taught to children as an equally valid way of life. However, religion is also an academic subject in its own right, involving the study of the doctrines, practices, ethical teachings, history and culture of one or more religions and with similar systems of assessment to any other school subject. At the same time, the subject is about personal development and has a more overtly moral purpose than other subjects in that it is intended to help children to understand what it is to have a religious commitment, to explore spiritual and moral issues, to develop a coherent framework of shared values and to reflect on the relevance of religion to the contemporary world. The subject is therefore well placed to take significant responsibility for the promotion of community cohesion which is now a statutory requirement (DCSF, 2007).

The content of religious education is thus a matter of concern to politicians, academics, teachers and parents as well as to the leaders of the main faiths found in the UK. However, if decisions about religious education are to be made purely on political, philosophical or educational grounds, the essentially secular approach to religious education that results may raise many issues for those who believe their own faith is the true one (as many believers do: why else would they cherish their own faith and devote time and attention to it?).

How should they respond if they find their children being taught that their own faith is no more and no less true than any other religion?

Diversity of different kinds has always been a challenge for religious education in the UK. The 1944 Education Act, the foundation on which all subsequent policy relating to religious education has been built, had the task of satisfying the requirements of people with a variety of religious beliefs, in this case Catholics, Anglicans and a range of non-conformists. It established a non-denominational form of religious instruction (as it was then called) for use in non-religious schools that was intended to be accepted to as many people as possible whatever their faith (and included a right of withdrawal for the remainder). The emphasis was on commonality rather than on diversity, with little attention being paid to differences between denominations and more emphasis on what they shared. This calls into question the common claim that religious instruction at the time was about religious nurture; it was more about creating a society based on Christian values, but the subject certainly did not nurture pupils in the distinctive beliefs and practices of their own denomination. The implied underlying principle at the time was equality of respect for all Christian denominations and the assumption of their equal worth.

Changes in practice in religious education over the last 40 years have continued to reflect the same underlying principles but have extended them to non-Christian religions (Copley, 2008). By the mid-1970s, the growing numbers of adherents of various world religions had reached a level in the UK (and especially in England) at which it was no longer viable to teach religious education based on the truth of Christianity, and a number of local authorities (notably Birmingham) introduced a new locally agreed syllabus which adopted a phenomenological or multi-faith approach. This new approach spread rapidly to all local authorities with significant numbers of non-Christian believers and fairly soon became standard practice across the whole country. The 1988 Education Reform Act reaffirmed the special status of Christianity among the country's religions but required local authorities to take account of the other principal religions represented in the country. However, current practice in religious education continues the tradition established in 1944 of playing down differences between religions and denominations, emphasizing commonalities and implying through its neutral approach that all are equally valid routes to an understanding of the divine.

The shift to a world religions approach to religious education, which Barnes discusses in more detail in this volume, parallels and draws strength from a theological shift towards religious pluralism. Of course, it has always been recognized that there is a plurality of religions in the world, but what has changed within the last 50 years or so is the growing belief that they are all in some way equal in their diverse understandings of God, transcendence, salvation and life after death. Pluralism also involves the related belief that such diversity should be welcomed, with the different faiths spending more time engaging in co-operation and dialogue and less in mission or evangelism (cf. Hick, 2001). In any case, as Cantwell Smith argues, the faith of others may not be 'so different from ours as we were brought up to suppose' (2001, p. 49). Pluralism is widely considered to be closer to the values of Western liberal secularism, more compatible with postmodernism and more able to discourage sectarian conflict and promote tolerance and respect. Pluralists are totally dismissive of exclusivism (i.e. the refusal to accept one's own faith as simply one among many equally valid religions in the world) and argue that exclusivism is fallacious because no one can fully know God, and in any case people are not saved by their knowledge (cf. Cantwell Smith, 2001, pp. 57–58). John Hull (2000), for example, criticizes exclusivists for trying to impose their beliefs on others and accuses them of 'religionism', implying that their sense of the superiority of their own religious beliefs can lead to prejudice and intolerance every bit as bad as racial prejudice and intolerance. Inevitably this leads to a counterargument that claims about the truth of one's own religious beliefs do not logically necessitate disrespect for those who believe otherwise. As we shall see shortly, Davis defends a more modest version of pluralism in the present volume, which he argues is perfectly compatible with taking religious differences seriously, and even with the 'confessional' approach to religious education adopted in many faith schools.

This brief contextualization of the debate has highlighted the need for a fuller critical examination of the form religious education should take in contemporary diverse societies and of the different political, philosophical and theological perspectives that lie behind decision-making in this area. Does pluralism provide the best basis for religious education to develop understanding of religious diversity and encourage empathy and respect for people of different world faiths? Or does pluralism, by blurring the boundaries between religions and emphasizing commonalities to the neglect of difference, provide children with a distorted view of what religion is really like? Since it is not possible for conflicting or contradictory doctrines to be equally true, is it disrespectful to the teachings of any given faith to teach religious education on the assumption of the equal truth of all religions? Does respect for others require an open and frank discussion of differences between them rather than brushing their differences under the carpet?

In his contribution to this volume, Philip Barnes fleshes out this brief summary of trends in policy and practice in contemporary religious education and argues that current models of multi-faith religious education in Britain are failing in their capacity to challenge racism and religious intolerance. Confessionalism has been abandoned in schools, he argues, for contingent reasons (like the difficulty of maintaining the approach when there are children from different faith backgrounds and none in the same classroom), not principled ones. Post-confessional religious education is regarded by its supporters as contributing significantly to the moral and social aims of education and is widely presented as being able to justify itself educationally on this basis. However, Barnes argues that multi-faith religious education has failed to realize its educational, social and moral potential, not because it has neglected the topic of diversity but because it has closed its eyes to the uncompromising nature of that diversity. A theoretical model based on the avoidance of indoctrination, neutrality between faiths and the belief that there is an essential unity and complementarity within different religions is used as a justification for the different methodologies that have dominated post-confessional religious education in England and elsewhere; but this model, he claims, is conceptually ill-equipped either to challenge religious intolerance or to develop respectful relationships between people from different communities and groups within society because it lacks the theoretical resources to affirm respect for persons alongside the intractable nature of religious difference. Rather than being complacent, religious education should therefore take difference more seriously and develop strategies and methodologies that are predicated on a true understanding of the nature of diversity, that confront prejudice and intolerance and that allow the voices of different religions to be heard, taken seriously and critically explored in the classroom.

In response, Andrew Davis offers a defence of what he calls a 'modest' form of religious pluralism as the basis for religious education. He argues that if equal respect is to be shown to all students irrespective of their religious beliefs, this means that religious education in the common school should not promote (or assume the truth of) any one religion at the expense of others. In any case, he claims, reasonable people do not seek to impose their views on others. While acknowledging the problems with the pluralist approach, Davis would not support any attempt to revert to an old confessional approach to religious education or any other form of religious education that is sympathetic to exclusivism and fundamentalism, because this might exacerbate inter-faith tensions, rivalries and intolerance. For these reasons he supports a form of religious education that is moderately pluralist and presents a number of arguments in support of this conclusion. The first is that different faiths normally focus on the same ultimate reality, even if it is conceived differently. The second is that conflicting truth claims are often based on a literal interpretation of religious language that is essentially metaphorical and therefore open to different modes of interpretation. The third argument is that holistic considerations provide an additional motive for rejecting religious exclusivism, because religions cannot be directly compared and therefore one cannot be found inferior to another: a religion is a holistic set of ideas and beliefs. In any case, religious exclusivism relies on an unethical concept of God who chooses some people, rejects others and keeps yet others in ignorance of the truth. He also argues that it seems unreasonable to believe that God has created a situation where only some people have the 'true' faith, whereas others have an inferior version of the truth or none at all. Finally, he argues that religious education should help students to see beyond exclusivism, recognizing that different interpretations of the same reality are possible and that religious pluralism encourages tolerance and social harmony. A strong, specific religious commitment is possible without the need to maintain the unique truth of one's own interpretation.

The whole debate is full of complex and controversial concepts that need the kind of philosophical clarification that the two main authors bring. In the Afterword, I provide further exploration of some of the central concepts, reviewing the main arguments and areas of disagreement and addressing some of the complexities that arise, as well as discussing some of the more specific issues arising in the debate itself. Since the authors do not themselves have the opportunity to respond to each other's initial arguments, I seek to offer some evaluation of the arguments myself in conclusion. However, it should be noted that the debate is far from an intellectual exercise that is removed from the daily practice of schools. On the contrary, it is a matter of urgency, for two reasons. First, it is apparent that in the foreseeable future the religious diversity under discussion is set to increase, not decline. Second, if religious education is retained rather than abandoned in the school curriculum, then pressure on the subject is likely to increase in the coming years to deliver commitment to the so-called shared values of British society, including tolerance and respect, and religious education teachers need to be confident that they are using the most coherent and effective way of achieving this goal.

Part One

Religious Education: Teaching for Diversity

L. Philip Barnes

The argument

What role should religious education play in societies characterized by religious and moral diversity? Religion is a controversial subject that divides opinion, and for this reason some educators favour excluding formal study of religion from public (or publically funded) schools. Such solutions are often advanced on the grounds that public institutions should be religiously neutral, though it would be unusual to hear educators also argue that schools should be morally neutral, even given the particular problems that attach to moral education in the context of Western democratic societies that are deeply divided on moral issues and on the legitimacy of competing lifestyles. The point is widely appreciated that there is no such thing as moral neutrality: any form of education, whether it includes explicit moral teaching or not, assumes moral commitments and transmits moral values. Increasingly, it is beginning to be realized that the same is true with regard to religion. Every form of public education, whether the study of religion is included in the curriculum or not, takes a stance in relation to religion and conveys a message about the nature and importance of religion. To deprive pupils of the opportunity to study religion in schools is not a neutral position;

instead a secular non-religious view of life is implicitly affirmed: the message is conveyed that religion is unimportant, or irrelevant to life or even too controversial to be studied. Yet in the real world of politics, public affairs and community relations, religion is both important and controversial. An education system that fails to advance a knowledge and understanding of religion fails to equip pupils to participate in civil society and contribute to public debates; in a real sense, it fails to equip them to become full citizens, where citizenship is interpreted not in narrow legal terms but as something active, deliberative and participative. Ignorance about religion can contribute to uncritical attitudes and in this way foster the growth of religious fundamentalism or it can contribute to overly critical attitudes that fail to take account of the diversity within religions and foster atheistic fundamentalism.

If a convincing case can be made for the inclusion of religious education in the curriculum, what form should it take? This essay presents the controversial view that religious education as currently theorized and practised in countries such as Britain and elsewhere is conceptually incapable of challenging bigotry and intolerance and of contributing to the development of responsible and respectful relationships between individuals and communities. It is argued that much modern religious education is indebted to liberal theological assumptions that assign religious validity and vitality to the different religions. This commitment, according to its supporters, ideally equips the subject to contribute to the moral and social aims of education that are appropriate to societies characterized by diversity and difference. Influential and popular as this position is (and acknowledging that it is often held implicitly rather than explicitly), it is unconvincing philosophically and educationally. It is this negative judgement that what follows seeks to justify, along with a concluding brief outline of the form religious education should take if it is to contribute to a truly liberal education that attends to the moral development of individuals and the social development of communities.

Setting the scene

The issue of how to accommodate diversity within the modern state and its institutions is central to contemporary political and social philosophy, particularly so in liberal democratic states that aim to be inclusive, participative and just; as Macedo (2000, p. 1) has commented, '[d]iversity is the great issue of our time'. Diversity is also central to much recent educational theory and policy, for clearly it is often in schools that children and young people from different backgrounds and communities are first exposed to diversity in a formal institutional setting. It is also in schools that the interests of the state and of wider society come to the fore as efforts are made to shape diversity for civic and moral purposes – at the very least, to shape diversity in ways that contribute to peaceful coexistence between communities and individuals with different beliefs, commitments, values and orientations. Educational policymakers and educators have to decide what kind of curriculum is appropriate for pupils whose parents (may) hold different beliefs and follow different lifestyles and what kind of stance schools should take on gender issues and on visual and symbolic representations of lifestyle and commitment in the school and in the classroom. There is also the important matter, already noted, of the role of education in advancing the claims of citizenship and furthering the aims of moral and social education. Such issues relate to educational policy in its widest sense and consequently require extended and detailed consideration, unfortunately of a sort that is not possible in this context; instead, the focus here will fall on the role of religious education in meeting the challenges posed by diversity to education and to schools.

By 'religious education' is meant the formal teaching of religion in schools (the appellation of which may differ in different countries), chiefly in public or 'common' schools that are intended to accommodate pupils from different groups and communities, but not exclusively so, for what is discussed will also be relevant to private schools and to religious or faith schools that combine education with some form of religious nurture. Increasing diversity in society raises questions about the aims of religious education, curriculum content, how religion should be represented in the classroom, methodology and so on. This narrowing of focus to religious education is less restrictive than it initially sounds, for the reason that the subject of religion in schools has often been the place where the reality and challenge of diversity to education has been most keenly felt, both because religious difference often subsumes other forms of difference, say, for example, ethnic, cultural and racial and because religion has historically been a major source of division and strife in society, and this has been reflected in debates about the role and the nature of teaching about religion in schools.

The challenge of accommodating religious diversity in Western societies, which in recent decades has thrown into sharp relief how religion should be taught and presented in schools, goes back to the birth of the modern nation state and how to deal with the divisive religious legacy of the Protestant Reformation and the ensuing 'wars of religion'. The Peace of Westphalia gave expression to the view that the religion of the ruler should dictate the religion of the ruled, as enshrined in the principle *cuius regio, eius religio*, 'whose realm, his religion'. In the seventeenth century, Locke argued that the state has no business interfering in the matter of religious belief, in part, because no individual who consents to government would think it appropriate to entrust matters of salvation to the decision of 'the magistrate'; in part, because other people are not harmed by the religious beliefs and practices of others; and, in part, because religious belief cannot be coerced. Enlightenment approaches to the political and social divisions caused by religion varied, though one popular strategy was to argue that the body of truth about God attainable by reason is sufficiently extensive of itself to generate a religion on its own; moreover, a rational religion that is directed to moral concerns and ends, as with Kant. The Enlightenment hope for a religion of reason to which all should subscribe and which education should endorse was hopelessly optimistic and floundered in the last century, both because the limitations and ideological commitments of 'disinterested' reason became apparent and because the increasing freedom granted by evolving liberal democracies to their citizenries resulted in, among other things, ever more varied and exotic religious expressions.

The emergence of public ('state') schools and state supported schools in the nineteenth century in Britain, America, and elsewhere, naturally extended the challenge of religious diversity in society to schools; schools that were increasingly mandated to provide education for all children and not just those whose parents could afford to pay or those who wished to avail of education for their children. How were those of different religious identities to be accommodated in schools and what kind of religious education was appropriate? Framed in this way, the challenge of diversity to religious education in schools invites a historical perspective – a perspective that is cognizant of the ways in which different systems of education have responded to the challenge of diversity and how schools have revised their aims and practice in dialogue with political, social and educational developments. Certainly, history has much to teach us in this regard, though not the kind of history that is a recitation of what has happened and records the facts of the matter and recounts how one strategy or policy superseded another, often retold on the basis of the unstated assumption that the line of historical development in religious education is one of inevitable 'progress' and improvement. What is needed is *critical* history that identifies the different commitments, beliefs and values that have historically influenced religious education in relation to diversity and then to subject them to analysis and criticism. The purpose of this kind of critical history is not to reach a fuller, more detailed understanding of the historical development of religious education but to learn on the basis of a critical reading of the past what kind of religious education is best suited to meeting the current challenge of diversity to society and to schools. How contemporary educators and religious educators in particular should respond to diversity cannot be divorced from how they have responded. A historical perspective is also necessary because it is often only on application in the classroom that ideas and theories reveal their strengths and weaknesses and that aims can be tested for their degree of realization; what initially suggest themselves to be good theories, when applied in classrooms often reveal otherwise. Some account needs to be taken of past 'successes' and 'failures' in framing new, more effective policies and practices.

The relevance of earlier historical developments and policies in religious education raises the issue of location and place, for there is no such thing as history or education in the abstract but only some defined period of history in a locality or some type of education in a specific context. Religious education is always education in a particular political, social and, above all, national context. This observation might seem to justify a thoroughgoing comparative methodology that attends to religious education in a range of countries and then to make positive proposals on a comparative basis. Such a methodology has obvious advantages but the detail (never mind the knowledge) needed to contextualize religious education in different countries, even before comparisons can begin, often goes beyond what is realistic. In addition, as in all other forms of educational research, there are inherent weaknesses in comparative studies of education, for the wider the range of comparisons made, the less confidence attaches to any positive (comparative) conclusions drawn. This is because different social, religious and political contexts so condition educational outcomes that what works in one place may not necessarily work elsewhere. Successful educational strategies and policies in one country do not necessarily translate into successful generic policies that are appropriate in all contexts. The best kind of comparative educational research, when pursued with the two-fold aim of testing different national policies and of identifying successful educational initiatives that are transferable, is when there are common influences at work, that is, where the same social, religious, political and educational influences obtain, for this gives support to the presumption that successful policies in one place can be successfully translated and applied in other contexts. To note this, however, suggests a further research possibility, which while producing more tentative conclusions than comparative research, nevertheless offers potential in relation to evaluating and framing educational policies that are widely applicable. This is to consider and assess policy developments and initiatives in one national educational context, which if chosen on the basis of its representative nature, may provide insights and suggestions for practice elsewhere. This provides a rationale for a case-study approach that attends in some detail to one particular national system of religious education, with the presumption that what emerges from a consideration of this one (representative) example is broadly applicable elsewhere, in other national contexts, given that the different systems are set in the same political context and subject to the same influences. A case-study approach is a plausible and intellectually defensible way of assessing and developing proposals and policy for religious education in societies marked by diversity and difference.

To which national context should attention be given? To answer this, a prior decision has to be made about which political context to consider, for there is a range of different ideological ways of ordering the nation state, its government and institutions and its citizens. Rather than seek to justify an answer to this, it is assumed in what follows that the overall political context in which religious education is considered is that of a liberal democratic state that aims to be participative and inclusive and engages positively with diversity. The focus will be on Britain, or more narrowly English religious education, for a number of reasons. Britain is a nation that has felt the full force of both modernity and late modernity – high levels of immigration, secularization, urbanization, the impact of globalization and so on. It has already responded to economic and social changes that are in some cases only now sweeping through other Western, post-industrial nations. The kind of debates in British education that result from increasing immigration and the emergence of more rights-based democratic forms of social and political involvement will inevitably have parallels elsewhere. In addition, formal religious education in Britain has a long (unbroken) history, going back to the early nineteenth century and the efforts of the churches to provide schools for the rapidly expanding urban population. From the early nineteenth century, religious education in schools has been in the forefront of educational debates, chiefly because it is regarded as the curriculum subject that most closely relates to and advances the moral and social aims of education, which in turn reflect the changing social and political landscape, of which increasing moral and religious diversity is a prominent aspect. For example, the practice of teaching *non-denominational* Christianity in state ('Board') schools and forbidding denominational Christian teaching, which goes back to the nineteenth century and the 1870 Elementary Education Act, is one early instance of British religious education confronting the challenge of religious diversity. The aim was to provide a form of religious instruction that was as inclusive as possible and represented the broadest possible agreement on the issue of religion in public education, in this case achieved by providing a non-denominational form of Christian nurture. British religious education has been and is engaged in a serious and historically extended dialogue with the challenge and implications of diversity for schools and for society.

This point leads naturally into a further reason why the response of British religious education to the challenge of diversity may be instructive to educators elsewhere: this is because British religious education is often portrayed and certainly regards itself as a 'world leader in religious education in public schools' (Miller, 2009, p. 6). The opinion is frequently voiced that responses to diversity in British religious education provide an example for other countries to follow – an opinion reinforced by recognition that British religious educators have been highly influential internationally. The writings of British educators, such as Grimmitt (1987), Hull (1982), Jackson (1997, 2004) and Wright (2004), are widely discussed and debated, and their ideas have inspired curriculum policy and reform in numerous countries. An assessment of the strengths and weakness of British religious education will have clear relevance to places where the British example is often viewed is indicative of future developments or where there is interest in policy developments inspired by British education.

The nature and challenge of diversity

The meaning of the expression 'the nature of diversity', and consequently its challenge to public institutions, is often assumed in social and educational literature and consequently the term is rarely subjected to close analysis. Part of my argument (in subsequent sections) is that religious education in Britain and elsewhere have largely pursued policies and developed methodologies that are ill-suited and conceptually incapable of challenging the negative reactions of some to diversity and this chiefly because there has been a failure to appreciate the nature of diversity and the ways in which diversity gives rise to prejudice, bigotry and intolerance. This misinterpretation is not helped by the focus of religious educators on religious forms of intolerance and bigotry to the exclusion of other forms. Let me explain.

In straightforward terms, diversity connotes difference or 'otherness' and the challenge of diversity is how to take account of difference in various contexts and places. Some writers regard diversity and pluralism as synonymous while others do not. The term pluralism and its cognates are more typically confined to social reality, whereas diversity, while applicable to social reality, is applied more widely. A different kind of distinction between diversity and pluralism (originally made in relation to religion) is drawn by the historian Martin E. Marty who thinks of diversity as a term to describe 'what is "out there" and letting it go at that', whereas the subject matter of pluralism refers 'to what people *do* with diversity' (2011, p. 9, his italics). This is a helpful distinction (even if it is not clear-cut) as it separates a descriptive understanding of human diversity from the uses to which diversity is put and the human consequences of diversity: implicit in this may also be a distinction between a descriptive and an evaluative or normative use of the terms. What people *do* with diversity in society, and how they react to diversity in society, are subject to moral and social evaluation; in this sense, pluralism corresponds to the 'challenge of diversity' – what we do with diversity and our approval or disapproval of what is done. The weakness of following this distinction, which is often seen in the writings of those who employ it, is that the descriptive nature of diversity is assumed to be straightforward and unproblematic. Attention is focused on the negative reaction by some to diversity in society – stereotyping, distrust, resentment, discrimination, intolerance, community tension, strife and division and on the factors or characteristics that are viewed as eliciting these reactions: religion, race, colour, ethnicity and so on. Accordingly, educational efforts are directed to challenging different forms of discrimination and intolerance. This of course lends credence to the importance of religious education, given that religion is well recognized as a source of intolerance. Religious education is viewed (or charged) with challenging religious discrimination, and as religions typically subsume other differences – ethnic, cultural, racial, which give rise to discrimination, so it is believed that religious education challenges other forms of discrimination as well. But what if the nature of diversity and what gives rise to intolerance are more complex than this interpretation assumes?

People differ from each other in an almost infinite variety of ways: people differ physically, emotionally, culturally, religiously, racially and so on, and people are also connected to each other in a complex web of shifting relationships of various forms of choice, contingency and necessity. Some of these connections and identifications are regarded as more important than others and some are more revealing (and even constitutive) of an individual's sense of self-identify and worth. Although diversity can be thought of in individual terms, as in a person's self-identity, personal or self-identity necessarily connects to social identify. None of us lives independently of others and who we are and who we perceive ourselves to be are conditioned by social relationships and social contexts. Society is made up of people relating to each other in a multiplicity of ways, sharing with others certain features of their lives, differing from others in certain respects, belonging to some groups and not belonging to other groups. We share interests and characteristics with others and we identify with these and with them; as the importance of these interests and our connections with other people increase, so we begin to identify ourselves (or indeed be identified by others) with certain constituencies and groups, sometimes formally and sometimes informally, consciously and unconsciously. Membership of certain groups becomes part of our collective and individual identities.

What constitutes difference, in the sense of which differences are regarded as significant by individuals and by society, is culturally and socially conditioned. Many differences between people are of no social consequence, within the context of ongoing relationships that are regulated by tradition, self-interest and convenience. In most instances, relationships between individuals and groups with different affiliations and identities are benign and positive, but on occasions in certain contexts, positive relationship give way to distrust, suspicion, bigotry and intolerance. There is a natural human propensity to classify people into categories and to distinguish between 'them' and 'us'. The denotations of these categories may remain constant over time from individual to individual and from group to group or they may vary, as identifications and commitments change. There are reasons why some differences assume importance in particular contexts and why some particular difference is perceived as salient, all other similarities apart. Individuals and groups are protective of interests and privileges, and clearly privileges and benefits that some groups enjoy (or are perceived as enjoying) can arouse hostility from other groups. Understandably, differences between groups, at points which are perceived as important and which are central to a group's sense of identity, have much greater potential to result in attitudes and actions that threaten the well-being and efficient functioning of society as a whole than differences between individuals. There is a competitive element to life and this competitive element takes different forms in different contexts. To this can be traced the roots of much division in society, though division in society can also result when there is no competitive dimension and simply arise where there is a perception of difference. In broad terms the more inclusive of identity the membership of a particular group is or becomes, the greater the depth of division that results when that particular marker of identity is perceived by its members to be challenged by some other group. This means that those viewed as 'minorities' and as having different cultural, ethnic, racial or religious identities can be perceived by the majority as a threat to society, simply because these differences are believed to express or signify differences that challenge the privileges, benefits, status and commitments of the majority ('indigenous') community; and to some, what is perceived as a competitive threat gives support to prejudice, intolerance and active discrimination.

Individuals and groups can come to be defined by a single characteristic and hence stereotypes are created. All other aspects of identity and commitment are overlooked and a common (often negative) identity with others is regarded as determinative of character and personhood and even worth. Individual identity is replaced by a single ascribed, collective or group identity. Often, the identity of others is classified on the basis of race or colour or religion and these become the single defining characteristic that elicits negative attitudes and behaviour from others; accordingly, distinctions are made between these different forms of prejudice. On this basis, *ad hoc* responses are framed to focus on a particular form of prejudice; for example, religious education presents itself as particularly suited to challenging religious discrimination and bigotry. The danger is that the (conceptual and linguistic) association between religion and religious prejudice tends to have the effect of detaching religious prejudice from other forms of prejudice and obscuring the fact that prejudice is not exclusively religious in origin and consequently that policies and methodologies framed specifically to lessen religious prejudice and discrimination are based on an incomplete and flawed interpretation of its cause and of the wider phenomena.

It is here that our earlier analysis of the nature of prejudice, discrimination and intolerance becomes relevant, for it alerts us to the point that ultimately discrimination and intolerance are predicated on the reality of difference. It is religious, cultural and ethnic *difference* that provides the occasion for intolerance: in an important sense, religion or culture or ethnicity are not causes of prejudice, they provide occasions for negative responses by some people or communities to difference. It is the *perception of difference* that lies at the heart of negative attitudes towards others. Use of the term 'perception' in this context is arguably interchangeable with 'reality' – for it is the reality of difference that lies behind negative attitudes towards others, in that the subject of negative attitudes and behaviour necessarily identifies some difference in the person that is the object of their disdain and resentment – the difference that elicits the negative attitude and behaviour is real to the subject. The challenge for educators is not simply to overcome the negative attitudes of some pupils to particular forms of difference, say racial, religious, cultural or ethnic, but to enable pupils to behave responsibly and respectfully towards those who are perceived as different, whatever form that difference takes. To think in terms of categories of discrimination and intolerance and then to form responses on an individual basis, as many educators do, fails to identify the true nature of diversity and the ways in which it gives rise to negative attitudes and behaviour.

Confessionalism and indoctrination

An obvious starting point for much recent theorizing and thinking about the role of religion in schools in relation to diversity begins with the premise that confessional religious education, which aims to commend and nurture some particular version of religion, is always educationally inappropriate. Here is a representative summary of some of these arguments:

(1) The educational goals of developing rationality and personal autonomy are incompatible with religious commitment.

(2) Religious commitment does not attend to evidence and proportioning of belief to the degree of evidence offered and is held independently of the relevant evidence and argument.

(3) No religious beliefs are known to be true and therefore they do not partake of the status of knowledge.

It is not possible to consider these arguments individually or even collectively in any detail, except to note a number of negative observations, which if capable of philosophical development, certainly blunt their force. The first challenge for critics of confessional religious education (or schools) is to provide a definition of indoctrination that applies only to religious nurture and its associated practices in schools and not to other subjects and practices, which are regarded as educationally appropriate. This is more difficult than it initially sounds. One popular definition of indoctrination equates it with transmitting beliefs without regard to justification and evidence; yet it is the case that children at a young age are frequently taught to accept beliefs and values long before they have the mental capacity to authenticate or assess the evidence relevant to their truth for themselves. In addition, there is no good reason why what is assumed or transmitted as knowledge at one stage of school education cannot be questioned and evaluated at a later stage: as pupils mature intellectually, so confessional education could take account of this and focus increasingly on providing them with the skills, abilities and knowledge to assess and evaluate religious beliefs. This may require confessional educators to integrate some form of (what for convenience may be termed) 'critical openness' into their teaching and practice to preserve educational integrity, though such need not evacuate the aims of religious nurture of meaning, import and application.

Sometimes it is argued that education employs rational methods whereas confessional religious teaching does not, and it is this meaning that is captured in accusations of indoctrination. This particular criticism, however, is open to the same rejoinder as the above criticism: non-rational teaching methods in schools are not exclusively confined to confessional religious education, for example, children often learn in schools by example and imitation or by sanction and punishment; this is even apart from the issue of whether confessional religious education needs to employ non-rational methods of teaching. A related criticism takes up the idea that (developing) rational autonomy is an important educational aim for all pupils, and one, it is alleged, that cannot be realized through confessional education. Is rational autonomy an essential aim of education? There are societies and there are communities within societies that do not regard rational autonomy as an educational aim: equipping individuals to be employable, morally responsible, take their place in the community and to contribute to the common good may be more relevant and defensible goals for educators. It could be argued that an autonomy based version of education wrongly imposes commitments on individuals and communities that are incompatible with any version of liberalism that seeks to be inclusive and supportive of democratic citizenship. There may even be a case for concluding that communities have the right to their own forms of education (within limits of course) and it is not the role of the nation state (or the influential political elite) to deprive schoolchildren of the values and commitments that are espoused by their parents and constitutive of their communities. What moral right has the state to impose its (no doubt ideological) version of 'the good life' on all citizens? More pointedly and specifically, for example, what moral right does a liberal democratic state have to impose one particular version of rational autonomy on Muslim pupils?

Historically, (personal) autonomy along with rationality have (individually or as combined) often been interpreted in ways that are inherently anti-religious and biased against religious forms of life. This animus toward religious belief is frequently indebted to and inspired by Enlightenment accounts and valorizations of 'scientific' or 'disinterested' reason, which are now widely discredited philosophically: scientifically inspired forms of philosophical positivism would seem to be the obvious example. This raises the issue of what is meant by rational autonomy; again, it is not at all clear that a plausible account of rational autonomy necessarily excludes religious nurture. To this may be added the point often made by religious adherents that commitment to religious belief and practice can enhance personal autonomy by freeing individuals from the desires, motivations and actions that impede responsible, self-directed decisions and behaviour; and it may be said, in Kantian fashion, that autonomy on this interpretation can be related essentially to moral practice. According to Kant, one is truly autonomous only when following the dictates of practical reason – in other words, autonomy and obedience to the moral law (of reason) are necessarily related: religion, to the degree that it enjoins moral behaviour, supports rational autonomy (though whether Kant's particular re-interpretation of religion is convincing in either religious or moral terms is another matter). The greater the detachment of rational autonomy from positive moral and social beliefs and behaviour, the more difficult it is to justify it as an essential educational aim. Moreover, there is evidence that suggests that religious individuals are more socially responsible and more law abiding than those who are not religious (see Stark, 2013). While the claim that confessional religious teaching frustrates and arrests the development of rational autonomy is conceptual in part, it is also an empirical matter; and the aim of advancing rational autonomy through education should be assessed in terms of outcomes and not determined in advance by controversial and disputed philosophical judgements. It is not at all clear (in empirical terms) that those who are religious are less rational or moral than non-religious people or incapable of making responsible self-directed life choices. What is the evidence?

One final point worth making is that the danger of religious indoctrination in schools is in all probability greatly exaggerated. This is because indoctrination is unlikely to be successful in liberal democratic, pluralist societies where contrary beliefs and worldviews abound and are widely publicized, and where individuals, for the most part, enjoy freedom of belief. Indoctrination, political, religious or secular, is successful only within a context where one particular set of beliefs and values is affirmed by (all) public and social institutions and where there is no independent realm of 'private' life where other beliefs and values can be espoused and practised. Religious young people in the West are exposed to a range of beliefs and lifestyles and some take advantage of the freedom they enjoy to renounce religious values and commitments transmitted to them as children. In the same way, some non-religious individuals brought up in a totally non-religious way, reinforced by secular schools and education, subsequently choose to espouse religious beliefs and practices. Religious indoctrination may work in totalitarian societies but not in liberal democratic societies.

These observations suggest that the aim of developing rational autonomy may either be inappropriate in all schools in liberal democratic, nation states comprising diverse ethnic, racial and religious populations with different interpretations of 'the good life' or should be reinterpreted in more educationally and philosophically defensible ways, which in all probability are compatible with religious nurture.

The objection that religious beliefs are not known to be true and to enjoy the status of knowledge, and therefore that pupils should not be encouraged to accept them, invites two contrary responses. The first is to question on what basis religious knowledge is denied. What concept of knowledge is assumed? There is a range of different accounts of the nature of knowledge canvassed by contemporary philosophers: internalist, say access or deontological internalism, or externalist, say causal or reliabilist. Which of these entails religious scepticism, yet commands widespread rational acceptance? The fact that some people do not endorse religious beliefs does not entail that they are not justified or warranted. Are there successful proofs for the non-existence of God? Is there *knowledge* that God does not exist, and is the case for a naturalistic worldview so intellectually compelling that pupils should be inducted into it in all schools? Clear difficulties attend providing a satisfactory and widely endorsed philosophical account of the nature of knowledge and of what counts as evidence in relation to religious belief, let alone proving that all religious beliefs fail to achieve the status of knowledge.

The second response is, for the sake of argument, to admit that religion is a species of belief rather than knowledge (in this context ignoring how these two concepts are to be related to each other) while pointing out that schools often inculcate beliefs and commitments whose epistemic status is uncertain and disputed: beliefs about human rights and their application, naturalistic or neo-Darwinian evolution, the moral propriety of homosexual relationships, the limits of personal freedom, the moral legitimacy of the nation state to impose sanctions and punishments on those who disagree with its evolving statutes, laws and 'burdens'. There would seem to be a range of moral, political and social beliefs endorsed by schools that fail to attain the status of knowledge. As this is the case, it is arbitrary (or discriminatory of certain groups in society) to exclude the transmission of religious beliefs as incompatible with the aims and processes of education.

The accusation that religious nurture is necessarily indoctrinatory has a long history in educational discussion and debate, with the late 1960s and early 1970s marking a period of intense reflection and writing on the subject. There are reasons, an outline of which has been provided above, which suggest otherwise. Less comfort, however, can be drawn from this than some religious apologists might imagine. First, as already conceded, it may be that religious nurture as practised in some contexts is educationally illegitimate and should be revised in ways compatible with a proper understanding of the nature of education. Second, in *Working Paper 36: Religious Education in the Secondary School* (1971), the semi-official document produced by the Schools Council that heralded the death knell of Christian confessionalism in 'state maintained' British schools, alongside the (unconvincing) argument that religious nurture is essentially indoctrinatory, was a further (as originally presented unsystematic) argument that challenges the propriety of religious nurture; this is a more telling argument, albeit up to a point; the qualification is important. This was an argument that was attentive to the particular constituency of modern Britain, more precisely to its multi-faith and value pluralist nature. The observation that modern Britain is religiously diverse, when combined with the liberal principle of freedom of religion, entails that the state does not have the right to impose conformity to any religious or non-religious creed on its citizens. Consequently, schools that are intended to accommodate all pupils ought not to proselytize on behalf of one religion. It would be educationally and morally inappropriate to use publicly funded schools, which are by intention and design open to all, to pursue confessional religious ends. Hence, confessional religious education is illegitimate. This argument rests not on the assumption that the state must be religiously neutral on all matters in all contexts, which may well be impossible in any case and certainly difficult to develop into a universal political principle, but on the social reality of modern democratic states, namely their religiously diverse nature. In a society where all individuals/parents do not subscribe to the same religion and where there is no widespread support for religious nurture in state schools, it is inappropriate. At one time there may well have been support for religious nurture in all schools (and this was certainly true in Britain up until the early 1960s), but this is not now the case. Some degree of opposition to nurture by non-religious parents may even be accommodated by allowing exemptions – where the numbers are small and where there is some measure of agreement in society that the social and moral gains that result from religious nurture in schools outweighs other considerations. In a situation where a large number of parents want to avail themselves of state education but for whatever reason (perhaps they adhere to a different religion or are simply indifferent to religion) do not want their children nurtured in religious faith, they should not be required to have them so nurtured, and for this reason confessional religious education should be abandoned. This is, however, a circumscribed conclusion and the argument does not provide a universal or normative justification for non-confessional religious education. What it does is provide a reasonable case, within the context of a multicultural and pluralist society, where different religious and non-religious viewpoints obtain, for the conclusion that state schools, which are by design and intention open to all, should not proselytize on behalf of one religion or 'comprehensive doctrine'. It does not establish the negative conclusion that it is illegitimate for any school within a multicultural and pluralist, liberal democratic society to pursue one comprehensive doctrine (nor does it illuminate in any way whether schools that pursue a comprehensive doctrine should receive financial support from the state or not). The contention that those who receive confessional education are considerably more uncivil, bigoted and intolerant of 'others' than those who receive non-confessional forms of education or no religious education at all *may* have some bearing on the moral and education legitimacy of confessional education, though it would require firm evidence to establish the point (evidence which may not be available, in light of some research findings; see Barnes, 2014a, pp. 19–22). In addition, in a democratic society people have the moral right to choose their own values and commitments and to transmit these to their children (albeit within limits), even though other people disagree with their choice of commitments and despite the fact that there is evidence that negative personal and social consequences follow.

The fundamental challenge for opponents of confessional religious education is that of establishing a *necessary* connection between indoctrination (defined in some way that distinguishes properly educational aims, methods and content from improper, immoral even, non-educational interpretations) and confessional teaching. If the connection is not necessary, in other words, if it is contingent, then confessional education can be revised and reconfigured in educationally appropriate ways. Some revision of current practice and content may be required by some confessional schools, perhaps accompanied by an acknowledgement that indoctrination happened in the past. This, however, would not amount to a repudiation of the aim of religious nurture, only the assurance that religious nurture in schools is now pursued in educationally appropriate ways. There is even a reason, internal to the practice of religion, why confessional educators should not aim to indoctrinate: this is because religions in general and Christianity in particular acknowledge that religious belief and conviction must be freely chosen to be religiously valuable. There is no *religious* merit in eliciting commitment to God if that commitment does not originate in the free decision of individuals, given that commitment that is compelled in some psychologically illegitimate or educationally indefensible way is without religious value. It may also be acknowledged that religious commitment brings advantages to religious institutions and to (some) religious believers – social, financial and political advantages, rights of representation and so on. All of these advantages broadly relate to the origin and exercise of power in society; and it is indisputable that historically religious believers and institutions have used unworthy methods to encourage religious commitment and obedience, from which they benefit materially. This is true of other individuals, groups and institutions in society as well – secular organizations, political figures, the nation state, school boards and so on. Illegitimate and immoral uses of power are not exclusively the preserve of religious believers and organizations.

It is concluded that the social argument against confessional religious education is *partly* successful. The qualification is important. It is successful in the sense that it establishes the case for regarding confessional religious education as inappropriate in certain types of schools, namely those that aim to be inclusive of different religious identities. It does not establish the conclusion that confessional religious education is inappropriate in all schools of whatever religious, cultural and social constituency.

The liberal theological model and religious education

Modern British religious education traces its origins to the rejection of confessionalism in schools and to its adoption of a phenomenological approach. Both commitments reflect the influence of *Working Paper 36: Religious Education in the Secondary School* (1971), which was written under the direction and guidance of Professor Ninian Smart of Lancaster University, who was the first head of a department of religious studies in a British university. His advocacy of a phenomenological approach to religious education reflected his support for the phenomenological study of religion and the idea that the study of religion should be neutral and objective. What distinguished *Working Paper 36* from earlier confessional accounts of religious education is the realization that social harmony will not be achieved by attempts to induct pupils into a common religio-cultural inheritance and that positive steps need to be taken in schools to challenge religious discrimination and bigotry and to foster positive relationship between different ethnic and religious groups in society.

The roots of phenomenological approaches (for there is no one single normative version) to religion are found in Liberal Protestant attempts in the late nineteenth and early twentieth centuries to develop a methodology for the study of religion that was more descriptive, broad ranging and neutral regarding the truth of religions other than Christianity; a methodology that was less driven by polemics in the service of Christian missionary expansion and more conscious of the agreement between religions and the divisive legacy of religion in the modern world. The intellectual context was increasing philosophical criticism of the 'proofs' for the existence of God (following Hume and Kant), the rise of biblical criticism, scientific positivism and Kant's radical moral reinterpretation of religion. In response, inspired by Friedrich Schleiermacher's appeal to religious experience as providing a credible foundation for religious knowledge (and no doubt aping Descartes' foundationalist quest for epistemic certainty), theology turned inwards to the experience of the divine within the self. Schleiermacher rejected Kant's twofold division of knowledge into pure and practical reason and in *On Religion*, he attempted to show how religion has 'a province of its own' ([1799] 1958, p. 21), distinct from metaphysics and morality. In later writings ([1830] 1928), he identified 'the feeling of absolute dependence' (*das schlechthinnige Abhängigkeitsgefühl*) as the peculiar form of consciousness that is characteristic of religion, wherever experienced. This feeling (or intuitive awareness) is the existential ground and (cognitive) source of religion; from it religious assertions gain their meaning and content, although beliefs and doctrines are derivative and secondary to the original experience and are as a consequence contingent and revisable. The heart of religion for liberal Protestants was, according to Lindbeck (1984, p. 21), located in the 'pre-reflective experiential depths of the self', and the public or outer features of religion came to be regarded as 'expressive and evocative objectifications (i.e. nondiscursive symbols) of internal experience'.

The reinterpretation of religion in terms of inner subjectivity and commitment brings obvious advantages to the liberal Christian apologist, for if the ground of religion is situated within the self in private experience, free reign can be given to criticism of the public aspects of religion. Effectively religion is removed from the realm of public knowledge and the realm of the sacred privatized; correspondingly, the public realm is secularized. Religion becomes concerned with inner experience and the hidden life of the soul and not with public knowledge or public life. Accordingly, religious knowledge is deeply personal, ahistorical and non-political. Such a reading of religion supports an easy accommodation with culture, for religion is withdrawn from the public world of ethics, economics and politics. The emphasis upon inner experience also creates the possibility of reconciling the religions to each other. If religious experience has priority over its conceptualization in beliefs and doctrines (following Schleiermacher), then the religions can posit agreement at the foundational level of experience, even though religious experience is expressed in different doctrinal ways. The original founders of Liberal Protestantism, for the most part, asserted the uniqueness of Christ (typically accredited to his teaching or spiritual receptiveness rather than his person), but recognition of the validity of religious experience outside Christianity increasingly came to be viewed by their theological successors as demanding a more positive estimate of the truth of other religions. If God is genuinely experienced in other religions, as to liberal Protestants his universal presence and omni-benevolence seem to require, then these other religions should be viewed as mediated God's presence and salvation. All the great religions witness to the presence of God in the world and his availability to be encountered and experienced in different cultural contexts.

In the early decades of the twentieth century, phenomenologists of religion appropriated the commitments of post-Enlightenment, Liberal Protestantism; indeed the emergence of the phenomenology of religion as a distinctive methodological approach to the study of religion is widely regarded as one important stream of modern, liberal religious thought. The aim of the phenomenology of religion, as professed by its practitioners, is to provide an objective account of religious phenomena, free from bias and distortion. The deliberate intention is to allow a religion, or more particularly religious believers to speak for themselves and record what they say and experience at face value; and then to move beyond description to grasp the meaning and inner motivation of religion. Religious knowledge gives way to religious understanding, for as one learns about religion and enters more deeply into the situation of the religious believer, so one comes to understand the nature and character of religion. The more one enters into the religious world of others, the more the universal character of religion as experience of the Sacred (or the divine) becomes manifest. This understanding of religion as developed and formalized by phenomenologists of religion such as Gerardus van der Leeuw, Friedrich Heiler, Mircea Eliade and others in the twentieth century gave rise to a twofold hermeneutical process. First, attention is given to the religious phenomenon under discussion with all prior beliefs and assumptions suspended (*epoché*); then in this focused state, the observer enters into the thought world of religion and intuits (through *eidetic* vision) the meaning of the experience for the believer. Characteristically, in phenomenology, the essential nature of religion is interpreted as experience of the divine – the Holy or the Sacred (the German, *das Heilige*, can equally be translated by either of these two terms): religion is regarded as a unique (*sui generis*) category of interpretation and knowing. Through empathy and intuition, the Holy is experienced and the meaning and force of religion is revealed: the 'objective' meaning of religion is laid bare.

The equation of confessional religious education with a 'dogmatic approach' and phenomenological religious education with a 'non-dogmatic approach' in *Working Paper 36* did much to commend the latter to teachers, as did the fact that the phenomenology of religion had already established itself as an appropriate methodology within the academic study of religion. *Working Paper 36* concluded that the phenomenological approach was the approach best suited to the promotion of religious understanding in a pluralist, multicultural society. Religious understanding and positive attitudes are conceived as two sides of the one coin. By suspending judgement and bracketing out one's own beliefs, one is enabled to enter into the experience of others, and in this way to gain a 'sympathetic understanding of the[ir] inner life' (Schools Council, 1971, p. 23): 'A Christian child can become a Jew for a day' (Schools Council, 1971, p. 26). Religious understanding is effected by abstracting oneself from one's own beliefs and values (*epoché*) and then entering imaginatively into the subjective life-world of others. Religious understanding and acceptance of others are linked: the more one gains an understanding of others by entering into their experience through intuition, the more one achieves empathy with them and values their perspective. This orientation provided a revised moral focus for religious education, not interpreted as formerly under confessional education as imparting and inculcating traditional moral mores but as challenging religious intolerance and effecting social harmony (see Barnes, 2014b, for discussion). Such a focus was believed to enhance its status and confirm its role as a statutory required element in the curriculum of all schools.

One can appreciate the attractiveness of the phenomenological approach to religious educators. Its descriptive nature and its purported objectivity were believed to distance teachers from the charge of indoctrination while simultaneously securing for the subject of religious education a fully educational foundation. It is multi-faith and neutral – no religion is privileged over another. Formally, the critical evaluation of religious beliefs and practices is set aside and bracketed out as the phenomenology of religion's methodology demands, so that pupils or students can enter imaginatively into the experience and 'Lebenswelt' of religious 'others'. In this way, one of the most controversial issues in relation to religion can be overlooked: that of assessing religious claims to truth and adjudicating between rival doctrinal claims. Religious education is freed from controversy and possible criticism. Phenomenological religious education also presents itself as ideally equipped to challenge religious bigotry and intolerance, for as one's knowledge and understanding of other religious traditions increases, so too does empathy and acceptance.

The influence of phenomenological religious education increased steadily in Britain throughout the 1970s and early 1980s. Its principles were enshrined in numerous textbooks, Agreed Syllabuses and Local Education Authority handbooks; its theological and philosophical assumptions were disseminated through numerous conferences for teachers and through the journal, Learning for Living, the leading professional journal in the field of religious education in Britain (in 1978, it changed its title to the British Journal of Religious Education). Here are a few representative quotations from influential religious educators of the period to illustrate the point that religious education, for the most part, uncritically appropriated the axioms and commitments of the phenomenology of religion (proper).

> ... the experiential dimension is central to religion and provides the justification for the other dimensions. It is this dimension which points us more precisely to the essence or nature of religion and religious belief.
>
> Religion ... [is] a unique mode of thought and awareness ...
>
> Grimmitt (1973, pp. 95 and 215)

> ... religion for all its many forms and manifestations is something basic and essential to what is human. The attempt to express this verbally also will, or at least ought to, emphasise that most of these forms are non-verbal. They are wordless because they are too deep, arising from the depths of the human and divine encounter. Even within the allegiance to one faith there are countless forms and expressions, and yet what gleams through the differences is precisely the unity of mankind in our primal destiny and in our relation to God. In practice students have quite spontaneously

declared that an understanding and respect for the religions of other men (*sic*) has deepened and clarified their personal faith within their own religious tradition.

Minney (1975, p. 223)

Phenomenology of religion … is concerned with a 'presuppositionless' approach to that which is essential and unique to the essence and manifestation of religion.

Marvell (1982, p. 71)

Marvell (1982, p. 74) goes on to recommend the production of new teaching materials that are 'evocative of the numinous', echoing the distinctive terminology of Rudolf Otto for the divine.

Despite its influence and popularity, however, certain weaknesses about the capacity of phenomenological religious education to further the social aims of education soon became apparent to teachers. The notion that acquaintance with the beliefs and values of minority religious groups by itself challenges religious bigotry and considerably reduces religious prejudice enjoyed little support from classroom experience. The second major criticism strikes right to the heart of the phenomenological methodology as propounded in *Working Paper 36* and in books and articles that applied and disseminated its principles. According to the phenomenology of religion and the phenomenological approach to religious education, an appreciation of others and of their beliefs and values is linked to the capacity to abstract oneself from one's own beliefs and values and then in this state to enter imaginatively into the subjective life-world of others. This process of abstraction opens the way to a deeper insight into the experiences and values of religions different from one's own. The problem is that a psychological perspective on children's cognitive development suggests that most pupils in primary schools are conceptually incapable of adopting a viewpoint contrary to their own (the evidence is summarized and discussed in Kay, 1997). At this stage of their cognitive development, pupils are unable to adopt a third person perspective on situations and experiences. The method of bracketing one's own beliefs and entering into the mind-state and experience of others in order to gain an appreciation of their beliefs and experience is undermined by the psychological and imaginative limitations of many pupils, in some cases, limitations that endure until well into secondary level education. This weakness should have been obvious to religious educators, for pupils in school necessarily lack the cognitive and intellectual abilities of university students and scholars of religion: a methodology that is intended to develop respect for religious difference among advanced students of religion was unlikely to enjoy an equal application to school pupils.

If classroom experience revealed that phenomenological religious education was less effective in challenging racism and religious bigotry than its first advocates had anticipated, this did not lead religious educators to question either the potential of religious education in this area or phenomenology's underlying Liberal Protestant theological and philosophical assumptions. The limitations of the distinctive methodology of religious phenomenology for gaining a positive attitude to those with different religious commitments could be acknowledged, but ongoing research that identified a link between notions of religious superiority and prejudice was interpreted by religious educators as confirming their commitment to the truth of the different religions and as viewing this as providing the best foundation for challenging intolerance. Respect for religious difference is properly predicated on belief in the truth of the different religions. In acknowledgement both of weaknesses in the phenomenological approach and of new developments, the term *phenomenological* religious education gradually fell into disuse in the late 1970s and early 1980s to be replaced by *multi-faith* religious education. Theological commitment to the essential unity of the religions remained.

The conviction that the different religions are each spiritually valid is constitutive of much post-confessional religious education in Britain. It was implicit in phenomenological religious education (as in Marvell, 1976; Hay, 1977) but increasingly explicit in later forms of multi-faith religious education (as in Johnston, 1996; Radford, 1999). Dennis Bates is particularly forthright in his identification of the theological roots of the liberal theological commitments of British religious education and of his support for it (see Bates, 1996, pp. 97–98):

it has been liberal Christian theologians and educationalists who were the major proponents of the study of other world religions in theology and religious education in Britain since the late nineteenth century; their rationale for this view was a belief in the university of the one God or transcendent reality who or which was the source of the religious experience of all humanity.

Bates (1996, p. 97)

Confirmation of the significance of this underlying commitment in British education has been expressed by the Dutch educator, Bert Roebben, who in a review of different approaches to religious education in Europe, identifies British multi-faith religious education with the theological assumption that 'God represents himself in different historically contingent forms of religious experience' (Roebben, 2007, p. 42). According to him, British multi-faith religious education 'legitimizes' itself on this basis.

A clear and programmatic expression of the link between liberal theological commitment to the truth and validity of the different religions and the contribution of religious education to developing respect between communities and challenging intolerance is found in the work and writings of Professor John Hull, one of the most important and influential religious educators internationally of the last 40 years. According to him, belief in the exclusive truth of (their respective) religion by adherents is identified as the cause of religious bigotry and intolerance; the solution to which is to educate pupils that religious truth is found in different religions and in the ways in which the religions make experience of the divine accessible in different experiential and cultural ways. Hull introduces the term 'religionism', to refer both to the view that one religion is true to a degree denied to other religions and to the attitude of superiority that expresses itself as intolerance towards adherents of other religions (Hull, 1992, p. 70). Religionism, he affirmed, is rather like racism – there is the racist belief that one's own race is better than that of others and there are racist attitudes that show themselves in acts of discrimination against individuals from other races. Hull is quite insistent that '[i]t is not enough for religious education to encourage a *tolerant* attitude towards other religions' (Hull, 1992, p. 71, my emphasis), instead it should teach that the different religions are not in competition with each other but rather complement each other; this interpretation, he counsels, should also become part of the self-identity and self-understanding of the different religious communities themselves: 'anti-religionist training should become part of adult education in every church and parish ... [and] for adults involved in the life of mosques, temples and synagogues' (Hull, 1992, p. 71).

More examples of this way of thinking could easily be multiplied. Commitment to the essential (experiential) unity of the different religions is the underlying foundational belief of much modern British religious education. This belief may be held explicitly, as by John Hull and those influenced by him, or implicitly, as by proponents of a phenomenological approach to religious education (and of experiential religious education, on which space has forbidden any discussion; see Barnes, 2014a, pp. 105–109). There will be teachers whose practice and pedagogy betray such a commitment, yet unconsciously so: in some inchoate way, a positive connection is made between respecting others and accepting the religious validity and legitimacy of their beliefs and values. Something like this is expressed in the following quotation from the head of department in an Anglican ('voluntary aided') secondary school:

> I would want them all [i.e. pupils] to realise that we all have different understandings [of religion] but *we're not wrong*, we're different, we come from different perspectives and therefore it is good for us ... *to respect everybody's believing system.*
>
> (quoted in Street, 2007, p. 125, my emphasis)

The unity of religions: A philosophical critique

For some theologians and philosophers, the essential unity of the different religions is the only reasonable conclusion to draw from acquaintance with the nature and distribution of religious experience and any kind of critical reflection on its implications. It is the purported rationality of this conclusion (and developing rationality is one of the central aims of education) that presumably convinces some religious educators that commitment to the thesis of religious unity should both be the default position in schools and determine classroom practice and pedagogy. Does commitment to inclusive education not similarly require an inclusive theology? In a later section, it will be argued that there are serious educational objections to this position, which are frequently unrecognized by its supporters. This section aims to show that belief in the essential unity of religions enjoys limited rational support and for this reason cannot (and should not) provide the intellectual foundation for the practice of religious education.

It is widely acknowledged that the chief difficulty facing advocates of religious pluralism and belief in the religious validity of different religions is how best to explain the diverse, and well-nigh contradictory, belief-systems proposed by them and their adherents. How can experience of the divine give rise to so many conflicting accounts of belief and practice (a feature that for some actually lends support to agnosticism)? There is limited consensus among the religions on the nature of the religious quest, human nature, the nature of salvation and the religious object; yet there are good philosophical reasons for denying the existence of a plurality of beings that all share the attributes of deity: there can only be one God. Belief in the thesis of essential religious unity both maintains and requires that the same spiritual reality is revealed and active to save in different religions. The significant differences between religions challenge 'the pluralist hypothesis' (Hick, 2004) that each religion reveals and initiates communion with the same divine being.

Why exactly do the different belief systems proposed by the various religions constitute a challenge to the pluralist hypothesis that each religion mediates the divine presence and communicates salvation? Quite simply, in analogous non-religious contexts where the same external object is perceived by different subjects, there is 'agreement' between the respective reports – this may initially be characterized as similarity of description, though it is more complicated than this, as we shall note. It is on the basis of agreement between descriptions of experience that entitles one to conclude that the same object is experienced by different people. Where there is agreement between different experiences by the same subject, or more appropriately in the religious context, agreement between different experiences by different subjects of different religious affiliation, one is entitled to claim that the same object is experienced, in the sense that one knows (or is justified in believing) that there is a common object experienced. It is similarity of description which (typically) gives to different sense experiences the presumption that they are of the same object, that is, that they have a common referent. It is not essential that descriptions be identical, or in some contexts all that similar, though differences between accounts must be explicable in terms of the peculiar nature of the object or the relative positions (in space and time) of those making the descriptions; in other words, lack of similarity of description need not tell against *agreement* between experiences if there are relevant reasons to account for this. Agreement between descriptions is a necessary condition for believing (on rational grounds) that different subjects are experiencing one and the same object, that is, that different experiences have a common referent.

The suggestion that adherents of the different religions, through their various religious experiences (which in turn contribute to their distinctive doctrinal belief systems) are encountering one and the same spiritual object initially seems improbable; precisely because there is no common or even broadly similar description of that object across the different religions. There is virtually no belief common to the religions. The different descriptions of the divine in the various religions tell against the conclusion that they have a common referent; the descriptions are not only different but in particular instances actually conflict with each other; what is asserted by one religion is denied by another. God is triune in Christianity; essentially one, to the exclusion of incarnation, in Islam; an impersonal absolute in Advaita Vedanta; and without form or substance in some schools of Buddhism. What is affirmed by one religion is denied by others. The case for (normative) religious pluralism collapses on the irreducible dissimilarity of the different religions. According to the canons of ordinary perception and experience, the essential unity of the different religious seems, from a rational perspective, unwarranted. It may be noted that religious educators who support the thesis of religious unity and regard such a belief as foundational to the practice of religious education in a pluralist society do not address this crucial matter. It is simply assumed or asserted that there is a common spiritual reality revealed through the religions. There are, however, theologians and philosophers who have attended to this issue and their arguments merit discussion.

Two strategies can be identified in the literature: the first is to find a measure of substantial similarity between religions at some point, and/or secondly, to account for, in the sense of explain away, religious differences so that a plausible case is made for viewing the religions as complementary. The first strategy appeals to the positive force of religious experience; the second typically appeals to two different considerations: the (alleged) ineffability (or mysterious nature) of the divine and the contextual nature of religious truth. These 'arguments' will be considered in turn, in reverse order.

It is commonplace among post-Enlightenment theologians to recognize that religious beliefs reflect the historical context in which they were originally expressed and subsequently interpreted; and this recognition is frequently extended to the level of incorporating whole cultural periods or regions. The implications of historical and cultural conditioning for religious believers have been variously assessed. In one interpretation, it simply involves a recognition of cultural diversity; nothing much turns on this, perhaps the need to translate religious beliefs into suitably appropriate cultural terms; beware of confusing regional cultural beliefs with what is intended to be universal religious beliefs and so on. Other conclusions that have been drawn from the fact of cultural conditioning are not so agreeable to orthodox opinions about the truth and 'superiority' of some particular religion or other. Some philosophers have so interpreted cultural conditioning as to conclude that truth in any objective sense is unobtainable, to the point of claiming that truth is culturally determined and there are no appropriate criteria of rationality to settle conflicting claims to truth, perhaps no (objective) truth as such. This position is really a veiled form of epistemological scepticism, and a view when carried through systematically seems obviously false and self-referentially incoherent. In any case, relativism of this form is unlikely to be espoused by religious believers, or even by theologians who (minimally) want to insist that each religion is appropriate to its own culture: this is because it effectively excludes the possibility of truth in any independent and significant sense which would give meaning to religion and the religious life. Extreme forms of relativism effectively deny knowledge, hence knowledge of the divine, and since such knowledge is the basis for the whole religious enterprise, such relativism is effectively excluded to the religious believer.

This means that the appeal to relativism by theologians of a liberal persuasion has to be handled with care and precision: too strong a version of relativism entails religious scepticism, too mild a version leaves theological orthodoxy, including the claim to uniqueness, intact. The philosophical task for those who affirm cultural relativism in support of the thesis of essential religious unity is to undermine exclusive (and particular) claims to religious truth while simultaneously leaving sufficient religious truth over to give cognitive significance to each and every religion. These are reasons for concluding that these two aims are incompatible.

The view that cultural differences account for religious and doctrinal differences is held by a range of philosophers and theologians, John Hick, Langdon Gilkey, Gordon Kaufman and Paul Knitter, for example. Not surprisingly their appeal to cultural relativism is set within a theological context, Christian in this case, and this context, contributing as it does to their conclusion, has to be appreciated. The following form of argument is frequently employed: my presentation of the argument is systematized and formalized to draw attention to its central features – essentially three premises from which a single conclusion follows. Thus:

(1) Religious beliefs are conditioned by culture.

(2) At least one religion is true.

(3) God is a loving God. Therefore:

(4) Each religion reveals the same God.

There is the outline of an argument here but it needs development. (1) is ambiguous, in that the extent of cultural relativism is not made clear. This can be overlooked at present for as attention is given to the other premises it should become clearer. (2) is relatively straightforward. It is designed to rebut out and out religious scepticism, by affirming that at least one religion is true. Furthermore, it does not beg the conclusion – the initial premise is that one religion is true – not all. This should obviously not be interpreted to mean that only one religion can be true, for this would prematurely invalidate the argument, rather at the outset the truth of only one religion need be presupposed.

According to the Christian theologian and philosopher John Hick, premise (3) on its own is incompatible with an exclusive approach by Christians to other religions; he actually speaks of a 'moral contradiction' between the belief that God is loving and the belief that the only way to salvation is the Christian way, with the implication (he believes) that 'the whole religious life of mankind, beyond the stream of Judaic-Christian faith is ... excluded ... outside the sphere of salvation' (1977, p. 179). Neither the matter of Christian salvation nor Hick's specific argument need detain us. In any case, those Christians who assign uniqueness to Christ may not be denying the possibility of salvation to all outside the organized Church but rather asserting that salvation wherever experienced is through Christ. As it stands, however, (3) needs development.

(3.1) God, being loving, would want to share his love with all humankind.

We might want to add further:

(3.2) God being all-powerful should be able to share his love with all humankind.

Presumably (3.2) must make provision for human freedom: freedom to respond or not to respond to God. The reception of God's love is conditional on a positive response to that love.

We are now in a position to draw out the logic of the argument and to clarify (1), that is, the extent to which religious beliefs are conditioned by culture. (2) and (3.1) together state that there is a loving God who wills to share his love with humankind, and this loving God is revealed (initially at least) through one religion. Of course this is acceptable to all Christians, not just pluralists who affirm the thesis of religious unity. It is only when (1) is added, and more particularly, interpreted in a particular way that the preferred conclusion (4) follows.

What way must (1) be interpreted, in conjunction with (2) and (3.1), to yield (4)? (1) must be interpreted in such a way as to exclude the possibility that one religion could be relevant to different cultural contexts, that is, cultural conditioning must be such as to exclude religious beliefs being relevant cross-culturally. It is only if (1) is interpreted in this way (let us now call it (1.1)) that the argument is successful; because otherwise one religion could in fact possess universal relevance. Thus a loving God wishing to reveal his love is incapable of doing so through one religion, because that one religion's relevance is confined to one cultural region, consequently a loving God is required to reveal himself through a culturally relevant religion. It is a small (if not an absolutely necessary) step from this to the conclusion that all the major religions reveal the same spiritual object, and this in turn entails religious pluralism.

But there are grounds for thinking that (1.1) is false. The claim that religious knowledge is so conditioned by culture as to be inappropriate or irrelevant to other cultures seems to be falsified by history, where for instance Christianity and Islam have crossed numerous cultural barriers, and by the facts of religious conversion, where individuals choose to renounce the religion of their upbringing and surrounding culture and choose to follow a different religion. Religions are not culturally conditioned (or more properly determined) in this way; therefore (1.1) is false. This is the reason for setting out the argument in a formal way, for it is only when the argument is broken into its constituent steps (and it is recognized that (1.1) is required for the argument to be successful), that its mistakenness is exposed.

The argument can also be criticized by showing that in any successful version (1.1) contradicts (3.1); in other words (1.1) effectively denies the truth or relevance of (3.1) to all cultures. One can further ask what are the grounds for believing (3.1)? To give support to religious pluralism, such a belief must be present in each religion, for otherwise those religions without such a belief in God's love (and I would suggest Theravada Buddhism is an example here) are deficient in this regard in their interpretation of the divine and consequently have something of central importance to learn from other religions. Once this is accepted, we are back at the issue of assessing rival religious doctrines, with no assurance that each religion will emerge with an equal claim to religious truth.

Yet the relativist case is not entirely lost. Rather than pursue the line that knowledge is so constituted by culture as to be culturally determined, a simpler appeal may be made to the explanatory power of the relativist hypothesis – that the differences between religions are best accounted for by corresponding cultural differences. The first point to note is that different religions have arisen at different times in the same cultures (e.g. Hinduism, Jainism and Buddhism at the same time in India), and very occasionally at the same time in the same culture (e.g. Rabbinic Judaism and emerging Jewish Christianity) thus overturning the argument. In addition, religions win converts in cultures other than their culture of origin and subsequently flourish in an 'alien' culture. The facts of historical and contemporary religious distribution tell against accounting for religious distinctiveness exclusively in terms of cultural accommodation. If there is no clear religious demarcation between cultures, then the hypothesis that a particular religion is 'appropriate' to a particular culture and the difference between religions accounted for by different cultural contexts is simply mistaken.

Second, this appeal to cultural relativism rests upon the priority of culture over religion, that religion (and the religious object) is exclusively adapted to culture. Is it not at least as plausible to believe that culture is, in part, determined by religion? A plausible case can be made for the view that religious ideas and doctrines through their social impact contribute to and shape cultures. Given this, the explanatory power of cultural relativism to account for religious difference is significantly diminished.

Finally, given the position we are considering, that religious difference are explicable in terms of corresponding cultural difference, then it follows that the spiritual object accommodates itself to the cultural context of its followers. The extent of this accommodation needs to be recognized and the argument followed through. The spiritual object in Christianity is triune, personal, an agent in the world and so on. In some versions of Hinduism, the object is beyond predication altogether; and in one important school of Buddhism (Theravada) the very term 'spiritual object' is inappropriate because the *anatta* (literally no-self) doctrine denies the existence of an enduring self or object, including the divine! Equally varied descriptions of the religious path and end (*telos*) are found: Hindus speak of successive rebirths of the same spiritual 'self' on earth; Buddhists admit successive lives but deny the continuity of the same self being reborn; Jews, Christians and Muslims allow for one life only.

Quite obviously all these beliefs cannot be true because some of them are contraries. A clear example is the Christian doctrine of God and the Buddhist doctrine of *anatta*: if God exists, the doctrine of *anatta* is false; if *anatta* obtains the doctrine of God is false, both cannot be true. It is such examples that challenge the pluralist hypothesis that each religion reveals the same spiritual object. It is often precisely to meet this challenge that the appeal to cultural relativism is introduced. To be successful it must account for *significant* religious differences in non-religious terms (as in the examples above). It is necessary to account for significant differences in non-religious terms because to do otherwise would be to root the differences and contradictions between religions in the deity itself; and an object which encompasses incompatible properties is an unlikely candidate for existence. Significant differences between religions have to be rooted elsewhere if the intellectual credibility of belief in the divine is to be preserved: such differences must be external to the deity, thus escaping the charge of internal contradiction, in this case rooted externally in different cultural contexts.

The implications of this appeal need to be explored. If all the places where religions differ significantly can be explained by reference to cultural accommodation, that is to say non-religious factors, then it follows that what is left (in common) should be explained in religious terms alone. The truth is, however, that religious differences are extensive: there is no single doctrine on which all religions agree. Once the religious differences are accounted for in terms of different cultural contexts, there is nothing left of religion; nothing common of religious significance remains to be accounted for in religious terms alone to give content to religion. What began as an attempt to account for rival religious schemes being somehow compatible with their having a common spiritual source (or referent) ends in a naturalistic explanation of religious belief; for if all the places where religions differ can be explained by reference to cultural non-religious factors, then nothing remains to be explained. A naturalistic account of religion is complete. What began as an attempt to reconcile different doctrinal interpretations ultimately ends in religious scepticism.

The second strategy that is used to explain away and lessen the force of religious differences is an appeal to the (alleged) ineffability or mysterious nature of the divine.

The term ineffability is derived from two in words, *in*, and *effabilis*, literally, 'not speakable', hence our English meaning, inexpressible, unutterable and indescribable. The word can be used in different contexts, not all of them religious or theological, though it is religious usage which exclusively concerns us. In religious contexts, it is invariably the religious object or certain religious (usually mystical) experiences which are regarded as ineffable. These two applications are naturally related: because some religious experiences appear to their subjects as beyond description, it is frequently thought to follow (and with a certain plausibility) that the object encountered in such experiences is similarly beyond description. There are other reasons which have prompted theologians to claim ineffability for God. Some regard ineffability as a consequence of God's infinity, others a consequence of God's transcendence: God so transcends human beings as to be 'wholly other'. Such language is characteristic of mystical forms of religion and is particularly characteristic of Rudolf Otto's interpretation of religion and the phenomenology of religion.

The argument in summary form is a single premise from which a number of entailments follow:

(5)   The spiritual object is ineffable.

This is equivalent to:

(5.1)   The spiritual object cannot be described in concepts or language, therefore;

(6)   The different descriptions of this object in the great religions are inappropriate, inaccurate or unreliable.

(7)   Because inappropriate, the difference between descriptions is of no consequence, that is, trivial.

Hence, the embarrassing differences are explained away. The argument is valid; and let us for a moment accept that the initial premise is true: the spiritual object's ineffability entails that religious differences are inconsequential. This is not the only implication for religion. Strictly speaking, ineffability does not admit of degrees; it is logically impossible for one thing to be more or less ineffable – something is ineffable if it cannot be expressed in language, in this case, the spiritual object cannot be expressed in language. Surely then, one must simply be silent; ineffability entails silence; nothing can or should be said of the object of religion.

What would a religion be based on silence? No creed, no beliefs, no religious instruction, not even religious practices, for such practices would have nothing to express. What is the difference between a spiritual object about which nothing can be said and no spiritual object at all? Given premise (5.1) no words can express such a difference. The success of the ineffability thesis in explaining away religious differences is precisely because (all of) religion is explained away. But an empty 'concept' of God is of no serious interest to religion, or morality or for that matter to anything.

If the ineffability thesis is true, then all distinctions and descriptions of God are equally invalid; this would include traditional religious and moral predicates like God exists, or God is all-good, one could with equal justification say that God does not exist or God is all-evil. Very few adherents of the main religions would be happy with such a conclusion; most would want to say that the ascription of existence and moral goodness to God is preferable to the ascription of non-existence and turpitude. The point is not just that adherents of religion do make assertions about God, suggesting that for some, at least, God is not ineffable, it is deeper still; basically if any (one) proposition of the form 'The spiritual object is x', or 'is better described in terms of x than y' (where x and y are predicates), is true, then the ineffability thesis is refuted. I would propose that one such proposition (of many) is 'God is love'; consequently, God is not ineffable. Further, given that words and concepts have an application to the divine, we are back at the thorny issue of the significant differences between religions and assessing rival descriptions (in the different religions) of the religious object – back at the point the ineffability thesis sought to deliver us from, that of explaining away religious differences.

There are good philosophical reasons, for discounting the idea that God is ineffable, but may he not simply be mysterious, say in the sense of being beyond human comprehension? We cannot fully understand the nature and character of God and we cannot fully explain the compossibility of his attributes; and we can admit that human language and vocabulary are not fully adequate to express divine fullness. Yet, some understanding of the nature of God is essential to religion for it to be relevant to human needs and concerns: any interpretation of the mysteriousness of God must leave room for the ascription of predicates (and positive content), otherwise God is unknowable, as are his purposes and plans. A 'strong' interpretation of any mystery that attaches to God may explain how human 'knowledge' of divine reality is compatible with rival accounts of God's nature, but at the cost of emptying the concept of God of content. The same logic attaches to symbolic and non-descriptive accounts of religious language: the more we interpret religious language about God as expressive (of human attitudes or emotions) and non-descriptive, the less we know about him. Such a God does not correspond to the God of the theistic religions, a God that reveals his character and nature (and much else besides) through revelation.

A more common method of accounting for the differences between religions is to draw a distinction between religious experience and (doctrinal) interpretations of the experience and accredit differences to the latter. Doctrinal disagreement is trivial when compared with experiential agreement; and this agreement between religious experiences is suggestive of a common referent, hence the vindication of the pluralist approach to religious truth. Is this appeal to experience convincing?

A number of points tell against it. In the first instance, religious believers report their experience in terms of their own particular tradition and claim to experience the spiritual object of that tradition: Christians claim experience of a triune God, Muslims claim experience of Allah and Hindus experience of Brahman. Further (and no doubt obvious to most), it is not that believers from different traditions describe the divine in the same way, say using predicates $a \ldots$ to n, and differ only on the name used to refer to it, as if the connotations are the same and only the denotations differ. Rather, the reported religious experiences are different, and the characteristics accredited to the religious object on the basis of experience different. For example, the Christian feels an ontological distinction between himself/herself and God, the Advaita Vedantist looses his or her identity in Brahman: the experienced content is different. The truth is that religions are as divided at the level of reported experience as at other levels.

Second, to look to experience for a resolution of the difference between religions betrays a misunderstanding of the role experience plays in creating and sustaining religious difference. This is implicit in my first point but it is worth drawing out. Religion is much more than beliefs about the divine (as above), it includes a diagnosis of human ills, a specified way of salvation, an account of the good life and so on, and most of this teaching is based upon and derived from religious experience. For the religious adherent, experience provides a justification of his or her particular religion and thus provides a justification for the very doctrines that divide religions. For example, the basis of Islamic belief is found in Muhammad's call to be a prophet of Allah, his subsequent reception and then publication of Allah's message. The distinctive doctrines of Islam find their origin in Muhammad's religious experience, and these doctrines are then authenticated in experience by other Muslims. By contrast, Advaita Vedantists find justification for a very different set of beliefs and practices in their experience; Buddhists, Jews and Christians do likewise. To look for a resolution of the doctrinal, metaphysical and ethical disagreements (not to mention disagreements over the interpretation, and even occurrence, of events in history!) between religions at the level of experience is to fail to appreciate the role experience plays in establishing such disagreements in the first place.

A critical response to this might be to argue that the above concept of religious experience is too broad, for it includes 'revelatory' or special experiences in which God is believed to communicate with chosen individuals, who are then tasked with sharing the message with others. Other religions that lack the notion of an actively communicating deity, as for example Theravada Buddhism and some schools of Hinduism, are apt to speak of (human) intuitions of divine truth. In either case the result is the same, an 'inspired' body of religious knowledge, usually at some stage committed to writing and received by those in that tradition as sacred scripture. It is in (competing) claims to special revelation that support is found for the beliefs and doctrines that are distinctive of the different religions. But surely agreement between religions can be found if one limits religious experience to what can be *immediately* apprehended. There are problems with this. In a strict sense, a finite human being cannot experience infinite qualities, and a religion confined to what strictly can be known on the basis of human experience would deprive the deity of the very qualities that qualify it as a fitting object of worship. Furthermore, such a restriction of the content of religion to what can be immediately experienced, clearly results in a truncated interpretation of religion from the perspective of the theistic religions, which have a clear doctrine of divine revelation. Advocates of an experiential reconciliation of religious differences are caught on the horns of a dilemma. On the one hand, a strict appeal to immediate experience justifies no present single religion, let alone all; on the other, a wider appeal to religious experience which allows for special revelation in order to give meaningful content to religion simultaneously re-introduces competing claims to religious knowledge and the desired reconciliation between religions seems further off than ever.

Finally, a distinction between religious experience and (conceptual) interpretation is often posited to facilitate the identification of a common experiential core to all religions (and thus advance the case for a common spiritual referent). Such a distinction is in all probability unsustainable. The idea that there can be religious experiences free from conceptual interpretation is widely challenged by philosophers of religion who have been influenced by the 'later' Wittgenstein (chiefly his *Philosophical Investigation*, 1958). According to him, human experience presupposes conceptual understanding, for it is in conceptual (and linguistic) terms that beliefs, experiences, emotions and feelings are to be distinguished. Experiences are structured and conditioned according to conceptual beliefs. In the case of religion, without the appropriate religious concepts and religious language, there would be no religious experience. Experience in general, and religious experiences in particular, do not constitute an autonomous realm of meaning that only subsequently comes to be symbolized in linguistic form, rather religious concepts and religious language structure and condition religious experience. Public concepts and language have priority over 'inner' experience. There is no private world of meaning and experience that either transcends or relates contingently to public discourse. This means that one's prior convictions and beliefs enter into and shape experience. Different conceptions of the divine enter into and shape religious experience: there is no religious experience common to the different religions and hence no agreement between experiences from which to posit a common referent.

At the beginning of this section it was conceded that a rational case could be made for the thesis of religious unity if it could be shown positively that different religious doctrines and experiences agree in a way analogous to the agreement between sense experiences of the same object or negatively if the differences between religions could be explained away satisfactorily: the appeal to religious experience attempts to do the former, the appeal to cultural relativism and to God's (alleged) ineffability attempt to do the latter. In neither of these cases is the argument successful. There are no good reasons for concluding that each religion refers to, and initiates communion with, the divine. This not a rationally compelling position but one beset with philosophical difficulties.

This negative conclusion has focused on the issue of reference and argued that there is a 'disanalogy' between sense experiences and religious experiences (within the terms of this appeal): agreement between sense experiences provides grounds for concluding that a common object is experienced, whereas the lack of agreement between religious experiences from subjects from different religions provides no grounds for postulating a common object. It can be acknowledged, as anyone familiar with debates in this area of philosophy knows, that there are difficulties with all general theories of reference – descriptivist, causal or whatever. Such difficulties usually take the form of showing how terms successfully refer while not fulfilling the criteria (or interpretation) of reference presupposed and required by some or other particular theory. Counter examples are provided that 'show' that the theory in question does not (at least) cover all cases of successful reference. In other words, there are reasons for concluding that particular terms refer successfully to actions, objects or states of mind, which the theory seems to discount or fails to explain. These counter examples reveal the inadequacies of a theory by showing that it fails to cover all instances of successful reference. General debates about reference, however, have limited application to the argument that is developed here against the conclusion that the different religions have a common spiritual referent. The argument here is that there are no good reasons for believing that the religions have a common referent (given the lack of agreement between descriptions) *and* that any further reasons provided to explain away rival and contrary descriptions, which tell against the claim of a common referent by those who affirm the unity of religions, namely the appeal to ineffability and cultural and religious conditioning, are also unconvincing. No general theory of reference is assumed, rather attention is given to the issue of how we know that religious or spiritual experiences have a common referent: which general theory of reference to endorse is irrelevant to this, as are attempts to exploit inadequacies and ambiguities in current general theories. The issue we are considering is specific and local. It is concluded that in the case of religious experiences we have no epistemic basis for affirming that subjects from different religions experience the same spiritual object.

The conviction that all religions are ultimately equal should not be privileged over other viewpoints in education and certainly should not provide the intellectual rationale and foundation for religious education in a pluralist democratic society that purports to be inclusive. If Christian confessionalism was inappropriate in schools because it attempted to foist on pupils a commitment and an identity that some did not share and that was contrary to the wishes of many parents, then it is equally inappropriate to use schools to inculcate a liberal religious identity that accords truth to all religions. It may also be asked why religious education in a pluralist democracy requires a theological justification, liberal or otherwise. Despite claims to neutrality by post-confessional British religious educators, the form of religious education that followed the collapse of Christian confessionalism in the early 1970s has been in some respects just as partisan and uncritical as that which it succeeded: if not Christian confessionalism, it is confessionalism of a sort, albeit liberal Protestant confessionalism.

Why the liberal theological model of religious education fails to promote respect for others

The representation of the different religions in education as essentially in agreement is not without its attractions. It is construed by some as consistent with the principle of equality; it is also believed by many religious educators to provide the subject with the intellectual resources to challenge bigotry and to develop respectful and responsible relationships between individuals and communities. The irony is that the (mis)representation of the religions in education as equally valid encounters with the divine contributes to the failure of British multi-faith religious education to achieve the social aims by which it sets so much store and to which it often (rhetorically) commends itself as making a significant contribution to the moral and social aims of education and to society. The simple fact is that many religious adherents do not acknowledge the *equal* validity of religions other than their own; and often these are the same people who take their religion and religious commitment seriously and who believe that claims to religious 'superiority' are required and justified by appeals to their sacred scriptures. To present the religions in education (or to assume for educational purposes) that there is essential agreement between the religions (and mutual recognition of the truth tracking nature of their experiences and beliefs) falsifies the view of traditional religious adherents. Such adherents may justifiably conclude that the nature of their religion and their particular religious commitment are not faithfully represented in education. They may conclude that there is no real respect for them and their values and beliefs, or appreciation of the fully significance of religious difference and diversity. Religious differences are minimized or explained away as unimportant and secondary in the cause of social harmony (ideologically construed).

The assumption that the religions are independently valid and complementary (and the educational methods and pedagogies that follow from this) actually undermine respect for others in a further sense. Consider the logic of the strategy. You are encouraged to accept adherents of other religions and to relinquish intolerance of them on the ground that their ultimate convictions are in agreement with your own. You adopt a positive attitude to 'the other' because the other shares a similar commitment to the divine. Acceptance of the 'religious other' is predicated on underlying religious agreement (in essential experience). This carries with it, however, the implication that no such respect for others may be forthcoming in those cases where there is genuine disagreement – no respect for those who resist the liberal theological temptation to view all religions as valid; no respect for the traditional believer, the agnostic and the atheist.

It is for this reason that current representations of religion in British religious education are limited in their capacity to challenge racism and religious intolerance: they are conceptually ill-equipped to develop respect for others where there is genuine disagreement. This understanding of the relationship of diversity and respect has the capacity to 'demonize' the other just as effectively as those religious adherents who believe in the exclusive nature of the truth of their particular religion. The boundary between 'insiders' and 'outsiders' may be drawn in a different place, this time between inclusivists and exclusivists rather than, say, between Muslims and non-Muslims or Hindus and non-Hindus, but the same binary distinction is employed. Respect for others is compromised when those who are to be accepted and affirmed must first relinquish any claim to uniqueness or religious distinctiveness. Religious education needs to move beyond liberal theological models that posit common commitment to the divine as the basis for respectfulness of others. Only when this is done can it engage fully with the reality and challenge of difference and diversity.

Up to this point our discussion has been couched in terms of developing respect for *others*; this is deliberate. Those who are familiar with British (and particularly English) religious education, however, will know that the usual way of conducting the debate about respectfulness is to speak of 'respecting beliefs and values'. The emphasis is placed on respecting religions. The 2004 National Framework for Religious Education (pp. 22 and 23), for example, refers to the need to 'develop respect for the beliefs and values of others' and of helping pupils 'to develop respect for their own cultures and beliefs and those of other people'. The focus of British multi-faith religious education is on developing respect for the different religions, belief systems and ways of life. The different methodologies aim to show the plausibility of religion and make pupils aware of its transformative power to change lives. In the phenomenological approach, for example, one is encouraged to enter into the experiences and life-world of religion and so gain religious understanding and come to appreciate the force and challenge of religion. Through employing this method pupils will also come to respect religion and the religious way of life; how better to justify respect for the different religions than to affirm their experiential power and (equal) spiritual validity! Unfortunately, this strategy emphasizes the wrong thing. British religious education seeks to develop respect for the beliefs and values of others, and in achieving this, it is believed, more positive attitudes are developed towards those who hold these beliefs and values. This places the emphasis of respect on the wrong place. Respect for persons has primacy over respect for beliefs. There is a strong case for concluding that respect for the beliefs and values of others is secondary and derived from the more basic notion of respect for persons. In normal English usage, it is more natural to affirm that we respect others than to say that we respect their beliefs and values. We respect persons, which is equivalent to saying that we acknowledge their worth. Persons have value; they have an inherent dignity. This is not a belief confined to those who are religious. It is a principle affirmed by different philosophies of life and worldviews, secular (Kantian, for example) as well as religious. We respect the beliefs and values of others because we respect them as persons. To respect a person is, *inter alia*, to be courteous, to listen to what they say, to take seriously their beliefs and values, to treat them in certain ways; respect for persons can also be enshrined in legislation, presumably equality legislation can be viewed in this way, opposition to the death penalty and so on. The fundamental point is that respect for what people believe and the actions and the attitudes that express respect are derived from basic respect for persons. We respect a person, and as a consequence we respect the views and opinions of that person; it is possible to respect a person and to think that her beliefs are false, or trivial or uninteresting. The problem for British religious education is that by attaching primacy to respect for beliefs and not to persons, it construes criticism of the different religions as disrespectful; and for this reason it has refused to engage with the issue of religious truth, even though pupils in a plural, liberal society are faced with a range of religious and non-religious options, from which they have to choose and to which they have to relate. There is no neutral religious position; choices are made, either consciously (preferably on the basis of knowledge, understanding and some acquaintance with the relevant criteria of evaluation and assessment) or unconsciously. British religious education has failed to appreciate that we can teach children to respect adherents of the different religions and those who profess no religious beliefs while equipping them with the skills and abilities to make a reasoned choice about religion. Equally, by devoting its educational energies to developing respect for beliefs and values, it has failed to engage fully with the complex web of inter-relationships between beliefs, attitudes and feelings that combine on occasions to encourage religious intolerance and bigotry.

Religious educators have developed strategies that attempt to minimize the significance of religious differences and weaken the boundaries between religions; attempts are made to remove the 'hard edges' of disagreement. Apart from being hopelessly unrealistic, this approach fails to appreciate the nature of diversity and the way in which diversity and difference can become a source of division in society. Religious differences are not the cause of bigotry and intolerance; religious differences become the occasion for the human manifestation of bigotry and intolerance. What our earlier analysis showed is that any difference can come to elicit negative attitudes and behaviour in some people in certain circumstances, though ethnic, religious and racial differences frequently attract negative attitudes and behaviour because they are particularly visible markers of identity, by which individuals and communities are distinguished. The solution for schools and education, however, is not to seek to convincing pupils that the differences between them are unimportant or insignificant, but to aim to develop in them the personal resources and dispositions of character to come to respect those with whom they differ. Respecting others and tolerating their beliefs and values are necessary social values in a pluralistic society where the reality and the challenge of diversity and difference are genuinely acknowledged. British religious education has failed to take diversity seriously.

Towards the future

Commitment to the essential unity of religions is often revealed pedagogically in the classroom by a focus on the similarities between religions, to the neglect of differences; by the use of a thematic approach intended to underline the common spiritual provenance of the religions; by the depreciation of the importance to religion of doctrine and beliefs (which are regarded as secondary and revisable interpretations of originally common or complementary forms of religious experience); and by explicit avoidance of both the contrasting truth claims of the different religions and the issues of religious intolerance and discrimination. What form should religious education take if it is released from axiomatic commitment to the thesis of religious unity? What implications follow for religious education, once the conviction that all the religions are in essential agreement no longer functions as a constraining (or controlling) belief that determines and conditions the content and methodology of religious education? The most obvious implication is that religious education will begin to take religious difference seriously. There can be open acknowledgement that the religions are different: they teach different things; they pursue different goals, they prescribe different courses of action and they recommend different practices. The reality of religious difference can be acknowledged, without the need to tailor representations of it to fit theological schemes that posit some deeper religious unity or to fear that recognition of real differences between people is somehow incompatible with respect for them. Of course, the religions have interacted and influenced one another, and they continue to influence and interact with each other; all this should be part of a pupil's education about religion. It is also true that there are theologically inspired liberal interpretations of religion that seek to reconcile them on the basis of a positive spiritual unity in the divine. Nevertheless, the religions are different in ethos and character; they have different accents and emphases. As the anthropologist Clifford Geertz has stated, 'they establish powerful, pervasive, and long-lasting moods and motivations in men (*sic*) by formulating conceptions of a *general order of existence*' (Geertz, 1985, p. 4, my emphasis) and religious accounts of the general order of existence differ. Post-confessional religious education in Britain has paid lip service to diversity by gradually extending the number of religions that pupils are required to study in the hope that by increasing awareness of religious diversity this will lead to a corresponding increase in respect for others. Following the 1988 Education Reform Act, Agreed Syllabuses were revised to meet the new legislation, and most prescribed a study of five 'principal' religions alongside Christianity (namely, Buddhism, Hinduism, Islam, Judaism and Sikhism). The Non-Statutory Framework for Religious Education of 2004 concluded that there should be 'opportunities for all pupils to study other religious traditions such as the Bahá'í faith, Jainism and Zoroastrianism' and to study 'secular philosophies such as humanism' (QCA, 2004, p. 12), a view endorsed by the more recent *Framework* produced by the Religious Education Council in 2013 (for review and criticism, (see Barnes and Felderhof, 2014). Requiring pupils to study over ten different traditions of thought certainly suggests itself to be a recipe for superficiality and confusion (see Kay and Smith, 2000; Smith and Kay 2000). Pupils must be exposed both to the seriousness and to the diversity of religions, but it does not take a study of over ten religions to achieve this. Familiarity with difference by itself does little to advance the cause of inclusion, a point appreciated by some of the early critics of phenomenological approaches in the 1980s.

To take religious difference seriously in schools is to acknowledge the importance of beliefs and doctrines; such an acknowledgement is also central to any responsible educational interpretation of the nature of religion. Beliefs are constitutive of religion and of religious experience. Christianity, for example, revolves around the concept of the Triune God who revealed himself in the history of Israel and sacrificed himself in the person of his Son to effect human salvation. Individuals become Christians when they come to accept the Christian interpretation of their existential needs and the Christian account of how their needs are met in Christ. To be a Muslim is to believe in the revelation vouchsafed to Muhammad and subsequently recorded in the Qur'an. A concern with beliefs extends to include the different ways in which beliefs are expressed in rituals, in art, music and drama, in history and in the lives of famous religious believers. Post-confessional religious education in Britain minimizes the importance of beliefs and doctrines, both in reaction to earlier claims of Christian indoctrination in schools and in order to divert attention away from the obvious differences between religions. Religious beliefs and doctrines are regarded as peripheral to religion, whose essence lies elsewhere in experience and encounter. Such a reading of religion is no longer intellectually credible; its continuing influence in religious education reflects theological commitments that are inappropriate to publicly funded community schools that are intended to cater for the wide diversity of personal beliefs and values that are represented in society. Pupils must be exposed to doctrinal diversity and the differences between religions; they must appreciate that religious beliefs are central to religion and that they are deeply and sincerely held. Respect for others entails accepting the other's right to believe something different, something that may contradict one's own beliefs and commitments. Disguising difference and failing to appreciate its 'intractable' nature only alienates traditional religious believers who take their beliefs and practices seriously.

A focus on the doctrinal dimension of religion also naturally raises the issue of religious truth, for the different religions teach different things and prescribe different activities. Pupils need to be equipped with the skills to reflect upon and to evaluate religious phenomena. Our society confronts young people with a rich kaleidoscope of religious ideas and practices, yet British religious education has resolutely failed to help them to develop a critical perspective that can recognize the arguments used by religions to defend their beliefs and practices and the considerations that are relevant to their assessment. At one level, British religious education attends to the issue of religious truth by insisting that truth inheres in all religions, but such a conviction actually fails both to engage critically with the issue of truth in religion and to equip pupils with the knowledge and skills to enable them to choose wisely from the rich variety of religious options that are culturally available. The implication of this is that there needs to be an element of critical analysis and critical thinking incorporated into religious education at secondary level, in order to provide the skills and the framework for assessing and evaluating competing truth claims. Religions typically do not claim to be relevant only to a particular culture or group. Their claims are objective and universal: pupils need to appreciate the nature of religious truth claims and the lack of consensus within Western societies on religion, and they need to acquire through education the skills and aptitudes to evaluate religion.

Any appreciation by pupils of the contested nature of religious truth must also necessarily take account of religious scepticism, which in the form of atheism can act as a cultural substitute for religion. Religious scepticism frequently provides the horizon of meaning against which religious phenomena are interpreted and assessed. Pupils need to be familiar both with secular challenges to religion and with religious challenges to secularism. There must be an open, dialectical and critical enquiry into religious truth, an enquiry that interprets and evaluates religious beliefs and practices from a range of perspectives.

Finally, religious education must engage consistently and comprehensively with challenging religious bigotry and intolerance. The respect that is shown to religious believers by taking seriously their beliefs and practices needs to be complemented by explicit challenges to religious and secular sources of intolerance. A range of arguments and considerations should be employed, philosophical, moral and religious. Use needs to be made of tradition-specific arguments and of the religious and spiritual resources within the different religions themselves, alongside arguments of a more general and accessible nature, and attention needs to be given to the relationship of religion to culture, the legacy of colonialism and both religious and secular affirmations of human dignity and human freedom. Religious education is much too complacent about the contribution it makes to social inclusion and to challenging religious bigotry and intolerance. Such themes need to be much more prominent in Agreed Syllabuses, textbooks, school policy documents and school practice.

A degree of humility necessarily attaches to any conclusions that are reached in this context, as it forbids either a full discussion of the issues or an extended illustration of the form religious education should take, once it is acknowledged that there is a need for change. A case for change, however, has been made by exposing weaknesses in current theory and practice in relation to the contribution of religious education to the social aims of education. Some positive suggestions have been added so that religious education can begin to fulfil its obvious potential in this area of the curriculum. The need for more effective strategies and policies in religious education to develop positive relationships between different communities is urgent, however challenging of current practice and policy.

Modern British religious education has failed to take religious difference seriously: difference has been 'domesticated' and reinterpreted as unimportant within a larger religious framework of agreement. The virtue of religious tolerance is rendered unnecessary in a world where all are presumed to agree ultimately. But all do not agree on the subject of religion and it is unlikely that all will agree in the future; we fail as educators if we do not prepare pupils for the real world where diversity abounds. Our earlier analysis of the nature and challenge of diversity alerted us to the fact that bigotry and intolerance are not vices confined to those who are religious. Moreover, they are vices that can be elicited by any kind of perceived difference. The educational challenge is to provide pupils with the moral resources both to tolerate difference and to respect those with whom they differ.

Part Two

A Pluralist Approach to Religious Education

Andrew Davis

Introduction

In my contribution to this debate, I oppose religious exclusivism and defend a 'modest' religious pluralism. I argue that educating for the latter is compatible with taking religious differences seriously and even with the kind of confessional approach still sought by many faith schools.

I urge that religious education ought to help pupils to understand something of the compelling reasons for pluralism. It also should enable them to appreciate just how damaging and destructive religious exclusivism can be, to appreciate that a strong religious commitment is compatible with rejecting exclusivism and to discern the power and humane character of a moderate alternative perspective. Barnes rightly notes that prejudice is not peculiarly religious in origin: nevertheless, a quick examination of the contemporary international situation reveals significant religious components in at least some of the conflicts, even if we concede that cultural tensions are often wrongly described as religious.

Religious exclusivism takes a number of forms. For instance, someone might hold that the God addressed by their particular faith is the only one that really exists. They would believe that the entities with which other faiths concern themselves are fictions. According to a milder exclusivism, the Divinity favoured by more than one faith is real; other faiths focus on the same real existent but their beliefs about his character are often false. Some think that Christianity, Judaism and Islam are related in this fashion. They see each of the aforesaid three faiths as dealing with one and the same real being, God, and each tradition as acknowledging this about their sister faiths. Yet each of them takes the others to be in possession of false beliefs about God. For example, the Muslim and the Jew deny the Christian Incarnation doctrines, while the Christian may dispute the 'Oneness' of the Islamic God. The Christian claims that Christ is the Messiah, while the Jew rejects this. Broadly speaking, exclusivists reject the idea that there might be more than one legitimate interpretation of the same ultimate reality.

My objections to religious exclusivism are bound up with support for a 'modest' religious pluralism. Comparing the doctrines, beliefs and practices of major world faiths reveals much variety and significant elements of apparent incompatibility. 'Modest' religious pluralism contends that, despite this fact, *many* religions *may* be focused on the same ultimate reality, referred to by some faiths as 'God'. Such a view differs from the fashionable global pluralism according to which all religions *are* 'about the same thing' and that everyone has their own route to the truth. Barnes argues against the latter type of religious pluralism, and I share his perspective here. I concede from the outset that some religions and cults may incorporate doctrines that are not true or defend moral sentiments that are abhorrent or both.

Many versions of religious pluralism and their associated objections to exclusivism have been linked to political liberalism. According to the latter view, a neutral state should be explicit in its refusal to favour any one religion. However, my arguments here make no assumptions about the appropriateness of such a view. Moreover, Barnes attacks the idea that the liberal goals of developing rationality and personal autonomy are incompatible with religious commitment. I agree with him – I see no incompatibility, though I will not be addressing that issue in this book. He also opposes the view that because religious beliefs are not known to be true, they should not be treated as knowledge in our dealings with pupils. I can only say that nothing in what I write here assumes any particular truth value for religious claims. Note that I do not intend to engage with any of the issues relating to phenomenological approaches to religious education in the UK. Barnes is critical of these, but the relevant debates are outside the scope of my treatment.

A defensible modest religious pluralism needs to explain how adherents of a variety of world religions could, in principle, worship or enter into relationships with one and the same God. For, they entertain differing conceptions of Him.

Moreover, we also need an explanation of how all those even *within* one faith such as Christianity can be seen as worshipping the same God. For, the diversity of ideas about God among the occupants of any one pew is staggering, though I can only offer anecdotal evidence. Some believe that God intervenes constantly in everyday events by, for instance, saving relatives from car crashes and by answering specific petitionary prayers such as those asking for healing. Others hold this to be impossible. Some are convinced that those who do not share their faith are destined by God for hell, while others think the opposite. More than a few still believe in 'Young Earth Creationism', namely, that God created everything around 6,000 years ago, while the majority see no reason to dispute the scientific account, according to which the universe is about 13.7 billion years old.

Furthermore, beliefs within faiths change and evolve; this is true even in the Catholic Church. For example, there has been at least a shift of emphasis between the Council of Florence around 1440 and the Second Vatican Council in the 1960s in the doctrine that there is no salvation outside the Church. Some have argued that we should not even speak of particular faiths, in the light of the sheer complexity and 'messiness' of beliefs; to satisfy concerns of this kind, I would be happy to follow the suggestion that we can replace talk of apparently unified faiths with reference to sets of truth claims (for instance, Ruhmkorff, 2013). However, for expository convenience, I will continue to refer to 'faiths' here.

The horrific impact of *salvific* exclusivism, according to which only those who follow one particular religious faith can attain salvation, affords a strong motive for opposing religious exclusivism more generally. Christians, Muslims and other faiths have sometimes supported salvific exclusivism. Moreover, there is a tradition even within Christianity that God 'saves' some but not others: ' ... mankind is divided between those in whom the power of merciful grace is demonstrated, and those in whom is shown the might of just retribution ... if all had been transferred from darkness into light, the truth of God's vengeance would not have been made evident' (Augustine, 1972, p. 989).

Yet salvific exclusivism arguably constitutes a moral scandal, at least as regards those major World Faiths that credit a deity with supreme moral qualities. The very idea that a loving perfect God would exclude from salvation those who, through no fault of their own, fail to adhere to any one faith, or any one denomination within a particular faith, is an ethical obscenity.

> No perfect, just God would lay down certain things as necessary for salvation and then give only some the opportunity to know of them. But any particular revealed religion, such as Christianity, has been known to only a portion of the human race. So no just God would lay down that knowledge of its teachings was necessary for salvation. (Byrne, 1982, p. 289)

Moreover, as expounded so far, this argument does not even attempt to take account of the possibility that elsewhere in our universe exist sentient rational beings knowing nothing of Christ, Muhammad or Vishnu and that these inhabitants of other planets would thereby be excluded from salvation. Some treatments of salvific exclusivism (e.g. Basinger, 1991) have thought of it as a particular version of the problem of evil. On such a view, one element of 'evil' would be the exclusion from salvation of every intelligent creature who, through no fault of their own, was never introduced to the favoured faith.

Although salvific exclusivism presents the greatest challenge to the notion of an all wise, all loving God, other forms of exclusivism also afford their own kinds of difficulties or manifest the 'scandal of particularity'. Moreover, in a view sometimes dubbed 'inclusivism', a Christian, for instance, may claim that their own doctrines need to be assimilated if anyone is to have the best access to God. 'Best access' sometimes refers to the possibilities of relating to the Divine in this life. At the same time, the inclusivist Christian in question may be kind enough to allow that others who do not 'know' God according to Christian tenets may still attain salvation. Evidently, inclusivism might be adopted by any World Faith.

All these religious stances imply a bewildering picture of an omnipotent, omniscient all loving God offering the business class route to Christians, Muslims (fill in whichever faith representative is telling us this story), while others have economy class at best. Barnes points out that even where a religion begins in one culture, religions are not culturally determined. In the contemporary world, boundaries are permeable. Conversions occur. Hence, we cannot argue that God is incapable of revealing himself through just one religion. We are, Barnes concludes, still in the business of assessing rival religious claims with no assurance that each religion will emerge with an equal claim to religious truth. My response is that we cannot even entertain the possibility that the truth of one religion excludes *all* the others without undermining the supposed supreme moral worth of the object of that religion. If there were arguments or evidence supporting the claim that one particular religion had a special claim to truth then this, paradoxically, would provide overwhelming justification for rejecting all religions other than those faiths that refrain from focusing on 'God' or 'Ultimate reality'. Examples of the latter include Confucianism and some varieties of Buddhism.

One common reaction to arguments of these kinds is to play the 'God is mysterious' card. We are told that God's ways are not the ways of Man – that we cannot judge God according to human standards and that the very thought of so doing is arrogant. God is beyond our understanding, and hence we just have to accept that He has ordained that one particular faith is THE route to Him. We are given to understand that if we refuse to accept this, we are setting ourselves above the Creator, who does what He does, and, so to speak, we had better get over it. There is a hint here of Calvin (1960) –'God's will is so much the highest rule of righteousness that whatever he wills, by the very fact that he wills it, must be considered righteous.'

Some decades ago, the Roman Catholic philosopher Geach (1994) expressed similar views: 'I shall be told by such philosophers that since I am saying not: It is your supreme moral duty to obey God, but simply: It is insane to set about defying an Almighty God, my attitude is plain power-worship. So it is: but it is worship of the Supreme power' (p. 70).

None of the positions outlined above, from exclusivisms to all-embracing pluralisms, make sense without realism about religious assertions. Alston (1995), offers the following version, where religious claims are 'true or false depending on whether some stretch of reality, some fact, exists (obtains) and is what it is independently of our attempts to cognize it – independently of our beliefs, theories, conceptual schemes, and the like' (p. 38). So, on the realist view, a claim such as 'God is omnipotent' is true if and only if there is a real God out there, and He is indeed omnipotent.

There have been attempts over the last few decades to offer reductionist/anti-realist construals of religious claims. The latter include Braithwaite's well-known theory (1970), according to which religious claims are not empirical and hence must be construed as expressing feelings. Also in the anti-realist camp can be found Wittgensteinian fideist accounts. These deny the existence of standards of rationality and truth independent of particular faiths or cultures. Hence, the latter cannot be examined according to such standards to see whether they capture an independent reality. Within such fideist perpectives, religious beliefs and assertions can only be assessed according to criteria embedded within the relevant faiths. (Needless to say, many have questioned whether Wittgenstein himself ever intended this philosophical account of the status of religious claims, but I cannot concern myself with exegetical questions here.) On a strong fideist construal of religious claims, no sense can be attached to the various exclusivisms. This is because the very idea of conflict depends on the possibility that religious claims are rivals in the attempt to capture an independent reality.

I am unable to offer evidence for religious claims being realist in anything like the sense sketched above. However, it does seem obvious that the vast majority of those claiming adherence to one of the major World Faiths take themselves as making 'realist' claims. *This is why exclusivism matters, and why, in particular, education about exclusivism should be regarded as a crucial element in an RE programme.* Religious people on the whole do *not* think, when asserting truths of their faiths, that they are merely expressing feelings. They know perfectly well others may not share their feelings about all sorts of things and that mere differences in feelings do not form the basis of a fundamental clash of outlook and values. So, it is the reality of worldwide realist construals of religions that matter here.

Liberalism and respecting difference

Barnes holds that 'it is possible to respect a person while at the same time being quite certain that their beliefs are false, trivial or uninteresting' (this volume p. 56). Behind his conviction, we can detect a classically liberal sentiment that commands wide agreement in the Western world. We live in pluralist democracies in which a variety of groups should be able to flourish in a condition of peaceful coexistence. The liberal is likely to believe that this is possible if we learn to pay each other the respect due to each individual in relation to their status as persons and citizens.

Barnes might feel that he could apply a widely discussed distinction between appraisal respect and recognition respect in this connection (Darwall, 1977). Appraisal respect is granted to someone because they exhibit some admirable feature. Thus, I might respect Hilary Mantel as a good novelist or David Hockney as an artist. Recognition respect echoes the Kantian thought that each individual enjoys a unique status as a person and is owed respect in accordance with this status. Thus, for instance, imbibed with this Kantian spirit we might hold that we owe persons recognition respect even if they believe in a God as possessor of features that we deny, worship an entity whose existence we dispute, or in a God lacking characteristics that we deem essential and so on.

However, I contend that Barnes's liberal vision is over-optimistic, to say the least. Let me explain. If my exclusivist construal of my religious faith means that I believe that other faiths are untrue, I may well struggle to pay adherents of those faiths appropriate respect. The contemporary international scene bears emphatic witness to these difficulties.

In support of Barnes, it may be objected that my suggestion of 'struggle' implies that I am working with an inappropriate understanding of the idea of respect. We should, the objection continues, follow Raz's understanding of respect where he observes: 'Respecting people is a way of treating them. It is neither a feeling, nor an emotion, nor a belief, though it may be based on a belief and be accompanied (at least occasionally) by certain feelings. It is a way of conducting oneself, and more indirectly, of being disposed to conduct oneself, towards the object of respect' (Raz, 2001, p. 138).

On Raz's view of respect, it is under an agent's control. I can decide how to conduct myself towards adherents of other faiths, even if I am an exclusivist about my own faith. While my feelings are not directly and immediately under my control, my conduct certainly is. So, when I oppose Barnes, I must be intruding an inappropriate element of feeling into my conception of respect, and that is why I am speaking of 'struggle' in connection with respecting other faiths. Yet, the objection concludes, this is to create a problem where none need exist.

It might further be claimed on Barnes's behalf, that some exclusivists have not been successfully educated in a liberal fashion and that this is the problem that needs addressing. They should be properly taught the value of affording every individual the respect that they deserve. If this were done, everyone could then be left in peace to pursue their exclusivist religious faith.

I would not oppose improving the way we educate students to respect those different from themselves. Yet this policy is unlikely to be implemented fully and successfully in the near future, and even if it were, I still maintain that recognition respect is seriously challenged by many versions of religious exclusivism. Raz's notion of respect, though cautiously expressed, seems to separate conduct too far from feelings and beliefs. Carter (2013) argues that the distinction between recognition respect and appraisal respect can only be maintained where recognition respect is accompanied by what he calls 'opacity respect'. 'Respecting agents, in this sense, involves taking them as given: not 'looking inside' them or evaluating their component parts in one's deliberations about how to treat them' (2013, p. 201). Recognition respect requires us to refuse to take account of the person we are respecting in any terms beyond their basic capacities as moral agents. My point here is that such a refusal is extraordinarily difficult to combine with an exclusivist perspective on my religious faith, even if it would be an ideal to which I should aspire. So here I am explicitly disputing Barnes's claim (this volume, p. 58) that we need not 'fear that recognition of real differences between people is somehow incompatible with respect for them'.

Divine transcendence

Realism about the Divine faces unique challenges because its subject is believed to be 'transcendent'. Why is this? Some faiths, such as Judaism, Christianity and Islam think of God as creator. This directly implies what I will call 'ontological transcendence'. Whether creation is thought of as an action somehow in time or rather as a relationship of ultimate dependence between everything that exists and God, it places the Deity in a class of His own. A profound difference between religions of India such as Hinduism and Buddhism, even where they contain important monotheistic elements, and the monotheism of the Judaeo-Christian and Islamic traditions, is the latter's emphasis on creation *ex nihilo*. Worship is the characteristic response to God in Abrahamic religions, while meditation and contemplation is prominent in Indian religions.

A second argument for transcendence makes most sense in those religions that focus on worship. Otto (1958) writes: 'The truly mysterious object is beyond our apprehension and comprehension not only because our knowledge has certain irremovable limits but because in it we come upon something inherently 'wholly other' whose kind and character are incommensurable with our own, and before which we therefore recoil in a wonder that strikes as chill and numb' (p. 28). Otto holds that only an ontologically transcendent God would evoke responses such as awe, fear and wonder. The 'grammar' of worship means that the object of worship must be supremely worthy of worship. Consider an entity that is restricted to properties that mundane items can also possess, even if it can possess such properties to some extraordinary degree. Such an entity seems to be less worthy of worship than a being whose nature incorporates elements that differ radically from the nature of anything else in existence.

Otto's reference to 'irremovable limits' also points to the divine being beyond our knowledge and understanding in some sense; I use the phrase 'epistemological transcendence' in this connection.

God, the theist feels, is so great that he is bound to be beyond our powers to know and understand Him fully. It would be appropriate to feel in awe of a being who was all powerful, all knowing and so on. However, there is a strong and persuasive tradition according to which we feel an even greater degree of awe, fascination and dependence in respect of a being who is also 'mysterious' – that is, to a degree unknowable because radically 'other' or 'different'.

Reference and transcendence

In this section, I defend a modest pluralism about the relationships between major world faiths by explaining in detail and arguing for the following: that faiths employing differing, conflicting and even seriously misleading descriptions of a transcendent divinity may, despite this, be focusing on the same being. So, for instance, the being referred to in Trinitarian terms by Christians may be the same as that referred to in Judaism and Islam in non-Trinitarian terms. So this thesis is in direct conflict with Barnes's observations (this volume, p. 40) when he writes: 'The different descriptions of the divine in the various religions tell against the conclusion that they have a common referent; the descriptions are not only different but in particular instances actually conflict with each other; what is asserted by one religion is denied by another.'

Theistic religions such as Christianity, Judaism, Islam, and, possibly some versions of Hinduism and Buddhism, involve beliefs about 'God' or 'Ultimate Reality'. In this section, I will not be concerned with religions that do not focus in any way on the transcendent.

Consider beliefs in general terms. They can be about, or of, physical objects, people, fictional objects, abstract objects, possibilities, numbers, states of affairs and much else. I believe that my house has a green front door. My thought is about, or of, an actual house belonging to me. Jones believes that the next door neighbour's daughter has blue eyes; Jones may be thinking about, or of, a certain girl who lives next door. Similarly, we have desires, hopes, expectations and doubts that may be about, or of, such items. Moreover, I might *say*, 'My father is 66'. Here, I may have said something about, or of, an actual man who is my father. I say, '4 is the square root of 16'. I have made a remark about, or of, the number 4.

Note two contrasting philosophical accounts of what it is for a belief to be of, or about something. The first springs from the descriptive-intentional theory of reference, held by Frege, and championed in the last century by philosophers such as Strawson, Searle and Dummett. And the second arises from the theory of 'direct' reference advanced by Kripke, Donnellan, Putnam and others.

The descriptivist explains how Jones's conviction that the next door neighbour's daughter has blue eyes can be of, or about a certain girl Jane, as follows: Jones thinks that there is such a person as the next door neighbour's daughter, and he holds that whoever is the next door neighbour's daughter has blue eyes. Finally, Jones's belief is true, or false, of that real girl Jane since she actually is the next door neighbour's daughter. Jones might *say* that the next door neighbour's daughter has blue eyes, and the descriptivist offers a similar account of when he has said something about, or of, an actual girl Jane.

What of the cases where proper names feature as subject terms in beliefs or utterances, such as Jones's belief that Jane has blue eyes? How might that belief be about, or of, an actual girl Jane? The descriptivist will invoke a community of speakers, within which the name 'Jane' has currency. The community, and Jones himself, must associate with that word a number of beliefs concerning Jane's features. Each member of the community will have a subset of these beliefs but there will be sufficient overlap between their selections for the name 'Jane' to have a clear use in that community. The actual girl Jane must possess 'sufficient' or 'most' of the properties involved in the community's cluster of beliefs.

Searle (1969), characterizes the beliefs in the above sketches as beliefs that such and such 'identifying descriptions' are applicable. He understands 'identifying descriptions' as follows:

At the extremes … (they) … fall into two groups; demonstrative presentations – e.g. 'that over there' and descriptions in purely general terms which are true of the object uniquely – e.g. 'the first man to run a mile in under 3 minutes 53 seconds'. Both the pure demonstrative and the pure descriptive are limiting cases ... most identifications rely on a mixture of demonstrative devices and descriptive predicates – e.g. 'the man we saw yesterday'. (p. 86)

The descriptive-intentional account of 'about' and 'of' would apply to Theistic belief and discourse as follows. Again, we need a speech community in which the term 'God' is associated with beliefs that He has certain features. Suppose, then, that Jones believes that God is looking after him. His belief is about a real existent God if Jones associates with 'God' those beliefs credited to God by his speech community, and a real existent God does indeed fit the beliefs in question.

This application of a descriptivist account of reference to God omits the expressions 'sufficient' and 'most'. In secular reference contexts, descriptivists may claim that 'most' of the beliefs that Jones associates with 'Jane' must be true of Jane if Jones's utterance 'Jane has blue eyes' is to be about or of Jane. In so doing, they imply that a looseness of fit is permitted. Searle's theory of proper names (1969, pp. 169–170) seems to allow this. His view of when Jones's utterance 'Aristotle was four feet tall' is of or about the formerly existing Greek philosopher comes to this: Jones associates with the name 'Aristotle' one or more beliefs of the form 'Aristotle is whoever is p'. Such beliefs will be selected from a disjunction of beliefs of this type whose members are made up from the beliefs of the community at large associated with the name 'Aristotle'. Jones must believe 'enough', 'sufficient', or even 'most' of the disjuncts, but we cannot, in Searle's view, be precise about just how many. Aristotle himself must answer to the descriptions concerned, or at least, to most of them.

Arguably, we ought to distinguish among those beliefs associated with 'Aristotle' and suggest that some of them are more 'important' than others. Achieving clarity about the notion of 'importance' is not easy. Could it be defined by reference to the beliefs most commonly held in the community in association with the name 'Aristotle'? Yet this may vary from one community to another and change over time. For instance, the beliefs that Aristotle's contemporary community associated with 'Aristotle' were not the beliefs that we, in a twentieth-century speech community, associate with that name. Ours might include: 'Aristotle is whoever tutored Alexander the Great' and 'Aristotle is whoever authored the Nichomachean Ethics.'

Another possible approach would be to identify 'important' with 'essential'. Then we might say that looseness of fit between beliefs and the putative referent of the belief or assertion should not extend to the object's essential properties. Surely, it might be argued, someone who wishes to have a belief of, or about, an item must hold that the said item has all its essential properties.

Suppose, for instance, that we were assessing, according to the descriptivist reference theory, whether Jones's belief or remark that Aristotle was four foot tall was of, or about, the formerly existing Greek philosopher, and that we ascertained that Jones failed to associate with 'Aristotle' the belief that he was a person (the property of personhood being, of course, an essential property of Aristotle). Or, imagine that, worse still, we ascertained that Jones believed that Aristotle was *not* a person. In such circumstances, we would conclude that Jones' belief was not of or about the formerly existing Greek philosopher.

The case of God affords a particular kind of challenge for the descriptivist account of reference. For example, Jones might think or say that God is looking after him. On the descriptivist account of reference, the following must apply for Jones's thought or utterance to be about or of God: Jones and his speech community must associate with 'God' a set of descriptions, and these descriptions must apply to a real being. Arguably, all the descriptions capturing God's essential properties must feature here.

However, God's ontological transcendence implies a degree of epistemological transcendence, as has already been argued. So any beliefs associated by Jones and his speech community with God cannot be fully known to be true. At least some of God's 'important' or 'essential' features cannot be known by users of the name 'God'. Epistemological transcendence does not seem to be compatible with a purely descriptive account of reference to God.

Now, the descriptivist approach to reference may well be correct when our beliefs and utterances concern fictional or abstract objects. If I believe that Heathcliffe loved Catherine, then my belief is about, or of, the character in Emily Bronte's 'Wuthering Heights' so long as the descriptions I associate with Heathcliffe fit a significant proportion of those attached to the fictional character Heathcliffe by Emily Bronte in the novel. If I think that Rawls's Theory of Justice is flawed, my opinion is about, or of, the relevant philosophical theory so long as I have a set of beliefs about it which are largely accurate. However, when it comes to things in the empirical world such as tables, chairs, people and planets, then a purely descriptivist account of reference is not adequate, and I shortly rehearse familiar philosophical considerations which should persuade us of this contention. Of course, a transcendent God is unlike anything else that exists. Yet I will assume in what follows that his existence resembles that of real objects in the empirical world more closely than that associated with fictional and abstract objects. The God or Supreme Existent on which many of the major World religions focus is held to interact with us – to be such that he can be the source of experiences and beliefs that are central to faiths. This places Him in an entirely different category from those to which fictional and abstract items belong. He is not an empirical object, but, nevertheless, causal interactions and relationships with Him are held to be possible.

I now outline two claims for which I tend to argue in detail. The first is that 'of' and 'about' come in a range of strengths and that the 'strongest' senses require the subject of the belief or utterance concerned to play an appropriate causal role in the generation of that belief or utterance.

The second claim may be summed up as follows: suppose Jones believes that Crippen is the murderer and that Jones's belief is, *in the strongest sense*, about or of Crippen. Both Jones and the speech community to which he belongs and in which, we are assuming, the name 'Crippen' has some currency, associate a number of other descriptions with the name 'Crippen'. In this situation, Jones's belief being about Crippen is compatible with some of those other descriptions being false or at least not being held with total understanding and certainty.

Several major World Faiths – Islam, Judaism and Christianity – think of their God as someone with whom they can in some sense relate and as an entity that can be causally involved in the beliefs and discourse of faith adherents. The situation is less clear in Hindu thinking. However, if it is appropriate to think of some versions of

Hinduism as theistic in any sense and to believe that Siva or Vishnu can enter into relationships with humans, then the same is true here as it is of the Abrahamic faiths.

I provide some justification for the thought that with causal links between God and Jones, a substantial 'lack of fit' between Jones's set of beliefs about Divine features and the nature of a real transcendent being is compatible with the possibility that Jones has beliefs or makes assertions of or about that transcendent being. 'Lack of fit' is not a precise phrase, but it certainly does not include a situation where there is no truth of any kind in beliefs about the Divine. If my argument is successful, it implies that where there is conflict between how different people refer to God, it neither follows that they cannot be referring to the same being nor that they cannot entertain beliefs about that same being. I turn now to my first claim.

Claim One: Of and about

The following extended example is inspired by Sosa (1970). Imagine that the tallest man in the world is named Lanky. He is a member of an obscure tribe that lives in the Amazonian jungle. His tribe has no contact with the outside world. No one in the world community, apart from his tribe, knows of his existence, let alone how tall he is. His tribe are perhaps aware that he is their tallest member, but they have no more grandiose beliefs about him, having no opportunity to compare his stature with that of members of other communities. Two doctors in New York discuss the medical characteristics that the tallest man in the world will have. They decide, for convenience and quite coincidentally, to refer to the tallest man in the world as Lanky. They elaborate theories about what other physical features very tall people will have – that they will have weak hearts – that they will have spinal defects, and the like. One of the doctors, Dr Jones, believes, on the basis of these theories, that Lanky has a weak heart.

Now if, *per impossibile*, the actual Lanky were to come to know that Dr Jones had this belief 'about' him, let us try to imagine Lanky's reaction. 'If I had not grown so tall, and my brother had developed the supreme stature instead of me, then Dr Jones's belief would have been about my brother and not about me. If Dr Jones's belief is about me at all, then, it is scarcely about me in any very strong sense. It is only if I myself am a causal factor (of the "right kind") in Dr Jones having that belief, that his belief can be about me in the strongest sense.'

We can now add details to the initial example, taking one step at a time, so as to steer it towards situations where the strongest senses of 'about' and 'of' prevail.

(1) A reliable report reaches the doctors that the tallest man in the world lives in the Amazon basin; a member of the Guinness Book of Records staff, McRosser, happens to be passing through the area – the first white man to visit. Though he measures Lanky's height, he has no time to take in any of Lanky's other details.

(2) As outlined in (1), but McRosser also manages to photograph Lanky and sends a print to the doctors.

(3) All the facts sketched in (1) and (2), and McRosser also goes to see the doctors himself and tells them of his encounter with Lanky.

(4) Add to the forgoing stories their consequence that Dr Jones goes to visit Lanky himself, taking with him diagnostic equipment. On the basis of the visit, he forms the belief that Lanky has a weak heart.

In all the situations (1) to (4), it seems fair to say that Dr Jones has a belief about Lanky or a belief of Lanky. However, in the example as originally described, only the weak sense of 'about' and 'of' is involved, whilst in (4) the strongest sense of 'about' and 'of is present.

It might now be objected that the stronger senses of 'about' and 'of' simply mean that the believer has *more* beliefs about something than in the weaker senses and that causal links between his beliefs and the object concerned are irrelevant. Thus, or so it might be argued, in (4), Dr Jones will have far more beliefs about Lanky than he would have in the original version of the whole story. I would agree that, as we move towards the situation as portrayed in (4), Dr Jones does acquire more and more beliefs. Indeed, this simply reflects how the thought experiment has been elaborated.

Nevertheless, I maintain that the objection under consideration still misses the point. After all, we could have imagined, if we had wished, that even in the situation as originally described, Dr Jones believed a large number of things 'about' Lanky – not only that he has a weak heart but that his toes are splayed in such and such a way, that his bones have such and such a calcium content, that his backbone has such and such a curvature and so on. The real Lanky would still be entitled, it seems to me, to make a response similar to the one suggested above. He can deny that the strong sense of 'about' is involved in the absence of causal contact between himself and the doctors.

Wittgenstein remarked: 'If God had looked into our minds, He would not have been able to see there whom we were speaking of.' McDowell (1980, p. 154), quoting Wittgenstein with approval, remarks:

> … rummaging through the repository of general thoughts which … we are picturing the mind as being, God would fail to find out precisely whom we have in mind. Evidently that (mythical) repository is not the right place to look. God (or anyone) might see whom we have in mind, rather, by – for instance, seeing whom we look at as we speak – seeing relations between a person and bits of the world, not prying into a hidden place whose contents would be just as they are even if there were no world – is (in part) what seeing into a person's mind is.

And at the end of the same paper he observes: 'One cannot intelligibly regard a person as having a belief about a particular concrete object if one cannot see him as having been exposed to the causal influence of that object in ways suitable for the acquisition of information (or misinformation) about it' (p. 162).

McDowell argues, in short, that speakers do not consult an internal recipe to see whether an object they actually encounter is that object about which they believed something.

Claim Two: Causal links versus descriptive accuracy in referring

We are now ready to examine considerations in favour of the second claim outlined above, to the effect that, with strong causal links between Jones and a given object, he can believe things of that object even if his grasp of its character is less than accurate. The less clear are the causal links, the more accurate must be the beliefs in question.

Donnellan (1966) famously and plausibly argued that someone who says 'Smith's murderer is insane' when reacting to a dreadful scene of death and destruction involving Smith may have no idea, at the time of speaking, about the murderer's identity. The speaker means to talk of whoever it was that murdered Smith. Now imagine that Jones is put on trial for Smith's murder, and we say, of Jones: 'Smith's murderer is insane.' We do not know it, but Smith committed suicide. Now if Jones discovers that we have said 'Smith's murderer is insane', Jones may well take our remark very personally. Despite the fact that the description 'Smith's murderer' does *not* fit Jones, we may still have succeeded in referring to Jones.

I do not think that it is possible to talk of something or have beliefs of or about that something if my beliefs about what that something is like are *wholly* inaccurate, however clear the causal connection may be between me and the entity concerned. In short, I hold that a comprehensive account of reference to 'real things' would combine descriptive and causal elements. I am going to have to assume that in this book: to establish it would involve extensive technical discussion about the theory of reference which takes me too far away from the topic of religious education and religious pluralism.

Suppose, as we have before, that Jones believes that God is looking after him or that Jones says: 'God is looking after me.' Imagine also that Jones associates with God a number of beliefs about His nature. Or that Jones's speech community in which the word 'God' has currency associated with that name the same beliefs about His nature. Then, even if some of these beliefs are not accurate, or even false, then, so long as the appropriate causal links obtain, either between God and Jones or between God and the speech community, then Jones can both believe and say things about, or of, an epistemologically transcendent God in the strongest sense of 'about' or 'of'.

I will not attempt to say much about the nature of the 'appropriate causal link' between believer, utterer, or speech community and God. Causal theorists in general have not found it easy to provide comprehensive accounts of so-called non-deviant causal chains in their characterizations of their causal theories of perception, knowledge, and so on. I can only offer sketches of forms of causal linkage that are at least prima facie plausible candidates.

It seems to be a coherent possibility that God causes beliefs in humans through ordinary perceptions they have of the physical universe and especially through their interactions with other people. If so, they might encounter God 'in virtue of' encountering people, objects, patterns of events, or whatever, – items which are causally related to God in an appropriate way. I follow Jackson (1977), in his discussion of the 'in virtue of' relation. A car is red in virtue of the body of the car being red. A car touches the kerb in virtue of some part of the car touching the kerb. Jackson lives in Australia in virtue of living in Melbourne. I see the table in virtue of seeing its top. I hear the aeroplane in virtue of hearing a thunderous sound. I sense the earthquake in virtue of sensing the vibration in my chair. Jones (perhaps) meets/encounters God in virtue of having a loving relationship with a friend or seeing a mother's relationship with her child. The 'in virtue of' relation need not be seen as 'reductive'. If it were, encountering God would be construed as nothing over and above seeing a mother's relationship with her child. That is not what is meant here.

It also seems possible that God causes beliefs of the kind in question through special experiences, of the type reported by mystics, or that God causes the beliefs 'directly' – that is to say, in the present context, that humans acquire the beliefs without having any kind of sensory experience, and God enters into the causal explanation of the acquisition of these beliefs 'in the appropriate way'. And there are further possibilities still, but I cannot explore them thoroughly here.

Knowing who God is

Alston (1988), was not persuaded by a Descriptivist Theory of Reference in the context of religious language. He suggested that 'God' refers to something in people's experience. Alston appreciates that 'something in people's experience' need be nothing like a *particular* perception or specifiable experience. Yet he also acknowledges that 'there must be some way in which it is communicated to others what entity it is to which the initiator was referring with 'God' (p. 119). He thinks that aspects of experiences within the context of a community of worshippers afford patterns of identifying reference that can be passed on – or, in the terms of this section, allow worshippers to 'know who' God is when sharing thought and religious discourse.

In more recent discussion (2005), he makes some comments that resonate strongly with the account I am developing here. For instance: 'If reference is primarily fixed by descriptions, then the attributes there specified define what it is to be God. And so, if an alleged referent turns out not to have such an attribute, that shows that it was not God to which we were referring. It's the attributes that call the shots (p. 231). He adds: 'If experiential reference is basic, then what is thus experienced is God whether he lives up to some favoured description or not… Experientially based reference makes possible a wider commonality between religions. Even if different world religions have radically different views on the nature of Ultimate Reality, they could all be worshipping the same reality' (p. 231).

Alston's account is incomplete, but I believe that it is along the right lines. I want to say some more about this issue, though my comments at best add something to Alston rather than 'completing' the story.

How, then can worshippers 'know who God is' where the God concerned is epistemologically transcendent? The points that now follow in effect rehearse once again the earlier examination of 'about' and 'of'. I draw extensively on Boer and Lycan (1975). Their discussion is long and complex; I provide my own simplified versions of their views where appropriate.

We may distinguish initially between two kinds of situations, type (a) and type (b), in which someone knows or fails to know who someone is.

Type (a): I first describe the paradigm examples, and then elaborate to take in less central cases. Jones can see Smith. If Smith is in a group, then Jones can pick him out from his fellows. Jones may say, pointing at Smith: 'I know who Smith is' (pointing at Smith). 'He's the son of the Archbishop.' Jones is not compelled to use a name – he might instead employ a demonstrative. 'I know who that man is (pointing). He's the son of the Archbishop.' Or, for instance, Jones hears two men talking in the next room. Again, he can say, 'I know who Smith is' (meaning the one with the high pitched voice that both he and his friend can hear). 'He's the son of the Archbishop'. In a variant of this he could exclaim, 'I know who that man is – the one with the high-pitched voice. He's the son of the Archbishop.' The name or demonstrative picks out someone currently being perceived.

Let us now turn our attention to more indirect forms of type (a) 'knowing who'. Jones sees Smith in a crowd and could have picked him out – the crowd was close enough for Jones to see each individual clearly and so on. We bracket consideration of whether Jones knows who Smith is – whether, that is to say, he could have pointed to Smith and said, for instance, correctly – 'I know who Smith is. He's the son of the Archbishop.' Instead, we focus on a conversation which takes place later. Jones still has a clear memory of the people he saw and can describe them individually. He outlines Smith's appearance to a friend, and inquires: 'Do you know who that was?' Suppose that the friend does know and can say something such as: 'That must have been the son of the Archbishop.' Then the friend knows who Smith is in an essentially similar fashion to the way in which Jones knows, if he knows at all, in the paradigm case initially described above. The friend knows who that man is: there is a causal link of the 'right kind' between the man concerned, and Jones's friend's utterance of the expression 'That man' which goes through Jones via his memory.

These remarks are, of course, more in the way of elementary appeals for a view of reference which includes a causal element. Such elements admit of great variety. The chain of causes from an individual to someone who knows who that individual is could be very extended and indirect. For example, Jones and his friend in the twentieth century could wonder who it was that Aristotle saw – if we imagine that Aristotle saw someone one particular January morning in Greece and recorded this fact for posterity. If Jones knows who Aristotle saw, this could still be, I would maintain, essentially a case of 'knowing who' resembling the type (a) paradigm.

Where Jones does know who Smith is in an (a) type situation, he will know something of the form 'Smith is the q', where 'the q' is some description or other. For instance, Jones might know who Smith is if he can say, correctly, 'That man is the Town Clerk', 'That man is the owner of the fleet of taxis' and so on. However, Boer and Lycan also deal with cases where descriptions are replaced by names. Suppose that Jones knows that Smith is Christopher. Boer and Lycan argue that ultimately this will not amount to Jones knowing who Smith is unless Jones already knows who Christopher is. For if Jones did not know who Smith was, and was told that he was Christopher, this would only help Jones if Jones already knew who Christopher was. Whereas, if Jones did not know who Smith was and was told that Smith was the son of the Archbishop (or that he answered to some other *description*), this might well be sufficient. Jones need not know who the son of the Archbishop is in any additional sense.

The idea is that something like 'Smith is the son of the Archbishop' will ultimately silence and satisfy a questioner who wants to know who Smith is, whereas an answer of the form 'Smith is Christopher' is essentially incomplete. Similarly, suppose that Jones knows that Smith is x, where x involves demonstrative reference to something being perceived or to something which was perceived. For instance, imagine that Jones knows that Smith is 'the man I saw last week down by the river', or 'the man Jane heard whistling at 2 o'clock this morning'. Again, there would be a sense in which this does not help Jones to know who Smith is unless he already knows, for instance who the man he saw last week down by the river is – that, for instance, he is the son of the Archbishop. Obviously, in some contexts, knowing that Smith is the man seen down by the river last week could well be said to exemplify knowing who that man is. I am not trying to restrict the uses of 'knowing who' but to discuss the characteristics in particular of type (a) knowing who. The essential incompleteness of answers of the form 'Smith is x' also shows up as follows: if Jones does not know who Smith is, where Smith is in clear view of him, it will not help Jones to know that Smith is the man seen down by the river last week unless Jones already has a satisfactory answer to the question: 'Who was the man you saw down by the river last week?'

The point not yet touched on is what values 'q' can take in answers of the form 'Smith is the q.' If Jones does not know who Smith is, an answer like 'He's the man with 10,000 hairs on his head' is unlikely to be satisfactory. I discuss this shortly.

Type (b): I turn now to a second type of situation in which Jones knows (does not know) who the son of the Archbishop is. In a paradigm case, Jones is confronted with a group of people and he wants to know who the son of the Archbishop is – that is, he wants to know which of that group is the son of the Archbishop. If he eventually comes to know this, he will be able to point perhaps to a certain person and say 'I know who the son of the Archbishop is. That man is.' Jones may have a name rather than a description in mind – perhaps he wants to know who Smith is – that is, he wants to know which one of them is Smith. This is not essentially different from the case where he wants to know who it is that answers to a given description, since he will hardly wish to know who Smith is unless he associates with 'Smith' at least one description.

We can describe more indirect cases of knowing who in (b) type situations also. For instance, Jones might have Smith describe to him occasions on which Smith saw various people, and Jones might wonder who was the son of the Archbishop. He might wonder, in other words, which of the people that Smith saw was the son of the Archbishop. He might eventually come to know that a certain individual, on the far left of the group of people that Smith saw down by the river last week was the son of the Archbishop. Boer and Lycan suggest that the most frequent answer to the question 'Who is the q' in (b) type situations introduce a name. 'Who is the Archbishop's son'? 'Wayne.' 'Who is the owner of the fleet of taxis?' 'Snodgrass.' But, they claim, though it is the most frequent answer it is essentially incomplete, relying as it does on people already knowing who Wayne or Snodgrass are (for instance) in an (a) type situation as described above. People will need to know at least one thing of the form 'Wayne is the p' or 'Snodgrass is the r.'

Clearly, the situations envisaged as (b) types, where the answer to questions such as 'Who is the son of the Archbishop?' involves pointing someone out will be relatively few in number. If we accept that the most frequent answers to questions such as 'Who is the son of the Archbishop?' introduce names, which in turn require knowing who in an (a) type situation, it is upon the latter that we should concentrate.

Before doing so, I will mention very briefly a third type of situation that Boer and Lycan discuss, where 'knowing who' features between descriptions. No names or demonstratives need appear. Consider just two cases: (1) Jones knows who the highest paid official of Puddletown is. He knows that the highest paid official of Puddletown is the town clerk. (2) Jones knows that the heir to the throne is the Monarch's eldest son. Clearly these are essentially general and need not be about existing individuals at all.

I would argue that it is necessary for the Theist to be able to know, at least in principle, who God is in an (a) type situation. We need to see why this is so. For, according to the position I want to oppose, we could know who Smith is in a satisfactory enough way by knowing that Smith answers to a certain set of descriptions. And if we could bracket off considerations relating to God's mystery, which I argued earlier militated against the descriptivist-intentional account of 'about' and 'of' in the context of belief and discourse about God, it might be thought that we could know who God is by knowing that He answers to a certain set of descriptions.

I can know who Othello is in the fashion presently being envisaged, certainly. Yet arguably, this is not a happy parallel. Could we not know who Moses was (is) in this way too? For the purpose of much discourse about Moses, it does not matter whether he is thought of as someone who really existed or instead as some fictional character out of the bible. So, up to a point we can know who Moses is in a similar fashion to the way in which we know who Othello is.

But once we are concerned in our discourse to talk about Moses as someone who really existed, things change. It must be possible for someone to know who Moses was in an (a) type situation when Moses was alive. In the paradigm case, they would have had him in view. Pointing to him, they would have been able to say, correctly: 'He is the leader of the Israelites' or 'He is the son of Amram.' Moreover, someone could know who P was in an (a) type situation even where no one ever knew that that man – that is, someone they could see or hear, or even, more weakly, remember seeing or hearing – was the so and so. Imagine that P was a hermit – his mother alone and unconscious during his birth on a desert island, dying immediately after giving birth to him. P lives his life in solitude on the island. After his death, when his corpse has been devoured by wild animals, passing archaeologists discover evidence that someone lived in a cave on the island. The clues available to them might point to the fact that just one person used to inhabit the cave. They might correctly be said to know who P was in an (a) type situation if they said: 'That man is the one who carved the pictures of animals in the stones at the top of the hill.' It would be true that their demonstrative 'that man' would not be causally involved in any direct fashion with the hermit P himself. But it is conceivable that there could be a more oblique causal involvement via the evidence left in the cave. So, the demonstrative expression 'that man' could be used to designate that particular man – the hermit – even though they did not have perceptions caused by the bodily presence of the hermit – even though they were not in contact, however indirectly, with anyone else who had such perceptions.

If the possibility of knowing who God is in an (a) type situation were unavailable, the case of God would resemble that of the fictional Othello or of an abstract object. God is, of course set apart from all other existents. However, echoing a point made earlier, the unavailability of knowing who God is in an (a) type situation would liken His ontological status to that of fictional objects and abstract objects rather than to the status of the 'real objects' of the universe, for example. This would, in effect, assign to Him the wrong ontological standing. To retain the 'concrete reality' of God, however different this may be from all other particulars, we must insist on the possibility of knowing who God is in an (a) type situation.

When the Theist knows who God is in an (a) type situation, he knows something of the form 'God is p', where p is some property. Yet persons are limited in respect of their knowledge and understanding of these properties.

I now argue that this difficulty is not insurmountable. Boer and Lycan put forward the view that knowing who someone is always includes a reference to a purpose – knowing who someone is for such and such a purpose. ' ... the question 'who is?' often leaves us in doubt as to what to say by way of reply. If our background knowledge about the questioner and the context of utterance provides no strong clues as to his purpose in asking, we will inquire 'Why do you want to know?'(p. 328).

If the purpose is locating Smith, then knowing he is the fourth son of the Duke of Puddletown is useless, whilst knowing that he is the man in the kitchen peeling potatoes may do very well. If the purpose was – to ascertain Smith's family connections – whether he is of common stock or whether he is of the 'quality', then 'He is the fourth son of the Duke of Puddletown' may be fine.

For what purposes do believers require to know who God is? Certainly not to 'locate' him, if God is thought of as omnipresent. The broad purposes concerned include worship, devotion and prayer. What is it, then, to know who God is for the purpose of worship and prayer? It might be thought insufficient for a religious person to have a limited grasp of the Divine nature; that for a religious person, to know who God is for the purposes in question would be to know all that must be true of God if He is to be an unsurpassable being. And since this is impossible, because an unsurpassable being must be mysterious, humans could not know who God is for the purpose of worship and hence could not worship.

This line of thought may be countered as follows: I have argued that the worshipper must think of the object of his worship as unsurpassable. Suppose, then, that to know who God is requires the worshipper to know that he is unsurpassable. Whilst this would mean that the worshipper must know that the object of his worship has a certain nature in virtue of which he is unsurpassable, it does not follow that the worshipper is required to have detailed knowledge of all the aspects of that nature. Perhaps a human being could acquire the belief that God is unsurpassable, with some appropriate causal link between God and that person, in a way which did not involve her in acquiring true and accurate beliefs about the entire divine nature and 'concluding' that the object of his worship, in virtue of such a nature was unsurpassable. I do not think, then, that there is any good reason to think that there is a sense of 'knowing who' from which a human is barred when confronted with the case of a mysterious God, a limitation which would prevent worship.

Let me sum up the discussion of this section. If we look at the ways in which different faiths refer to 'God' or 'the ultimate reality', we see a bewildering variety of descriptions being employed and also many cases of apparent conflict between the descriptions used by one faith and those used by another. If an exclusively descriptivist account of reference is correct, then Barnes would be right to claim that faiths employing conflicting descriptions of the divine cannot be focusing on the same God. However, once we appreciate that a causal component needs to be incorporated into an account of divine reference, we also understand that such reference is compatible with the use of at least some descriptions that may not be fully applicable or may even be not true of Him at all. If reference to the same being is possible even where misleading descriptions are involved, there is significant scope for apparent incompatibility between such descriptions. There are an indefinitely large number of ways of failing to capture the nature of the divine. This, then, allows for the possibility that different faiths can, despite the appearance of conflict, succeed in referring to and focusing on the same God. Nevertheless, we are *only* speaking of possibilities. Apparent conflict may sometimes turn out to be real conflict here.

Language about transcendence is not literal

I now explain and justify the thought that when the characteristics attributed to the divine by one faith apparently conflict with the characteristics credited by another faith, this does *not* necessarily imply that either one or both of the characteristics do not apply. Barnes asks how experience of the divine can possibly give rise to so many conflicting accounts of belief and practice. One way of summing up the burden of both claims here is that a transcendent and mysterious being *inevitably would give rise to such conflict.* Or, as Anderson (2005, pp. 154–155) puts it:

> According to the doctrine of divine incomprehensibility, although we can know God partially we can never know Him exhaustively; indeed, the difference between Creator and creature is of such magnitude that what little we do understand of God is but a drop in the ocean compared to God's self-under-standing. If such is the case (as most Christians would be inclined to grant) should we really expect our systematizations of what God has revealed to us about Himself by way of limited human language, grounded in immanent experience, to be logically perspicuous at every point?

Believers attribute a variety of features to 'God' or 'Ultimate Reality', and, on the face of it, their attributions are often in conflict. I now argue that because at least some language about transcendence is compelled by the nature of its subject matter to depart from the literal, it follows that apparent conflict is not *necessarily* real conflict. As with the discussion of reference, it needs to be emphasized that this element in a modest religious pluralism does *not* mean that whatever the character of the apparent conflict, there is no real underlying conflict. Cases still need to be examined on their particular merits.

Moreover, Barnes identifies a strategy designed to explain away and lessen the force of religious differences. He understands this strategy to be an appeal to the ineffability or mysterious character of the divine (see p. 41 this volume). He is surely right to reject this kind of move, at least in its most extreme version, since, as he points out, 'some understanding of the nature of God is essential to religion for it to be relevant to human needs and concerns'. (p. 49 this volume). My discussion of non-literal religious language, whatever its strengths and weaknesses, is intended to explore a way of handling apparent conflicts between the concepts and languages of different religious believers that is less extreme than the target of Barnes's attack.

There is, of course, a very long tradition in religious thought according to which at least some discourse about the Divine is not and cannot be 'literal'. I must emphasize the word 'some', since it is obvious that there *can* be literal language about the Divine. Note some obvious cases. First, consider the limitless possibilities in the form of negative claims. 'God will never cease to exist', 'God does not possess a physical body' and 'God did not take out a pen and write the books in the New Testament' are obvious examples. Negative *relational* claims about God can be literal too. Examples include 'God is not two miles away from Durham', 'God is not smaller than the Taj Mahal.' It is hard to imagine contexts in which such claims would have any point, but that is by the way. It may be difficult to provide robust criteria for distinguishing between 'positive' and 'negative' claims. 'God is immaterial' may reasonably be construed 'positively, and this looks like a literal claim. Nevertheless, it might also be read 'negatively', as meaning that God is not material.

Theology frequently offers *abstract* claims about God, and at least some of these positive examples also appear to retain their literal force in the teeth of Divine Transcendence. The many examples include 'God is Being', 'God is All-perfection', 'God's Existence is His Essence', 'God is a necessary Being' or even 'God's positive nature is such that it cannot be spoken of in literal terms.' Nevertheless, figurative language is often to be found embedded in the abstractions. Consider, for instance 'God is the Ground of our Being' and 'God is beyond the Universe.'

Distinguishing between the literal and the figurative uses of language is complex and contested. The realm of the figurative contains many differing types of linguistic riches. For the purposes of what follows, I will speak broadly of the figurative, and of the metaphorical in particular, by way of contrast with the literal. I understand that the former uses of language sometimes involve likening two things when in our normal and conventional thinking we do not see them as resembling each other. Thus 'Sally is a block of ice' likens Sally to ice, when a person simply is not like frozen water in the normal way of thinking. 'Juliet is the sun' similarly asserts a resemblance between a human being and a modest sized star.

To speak of a transcendent entity, we sometimes use language that in some way draws attention to a resemblance between a mundane item on the one hand and God or the ultimate reality on the other. Consider an assertion about God, say: 'God is a person.' It carries at least an implication that there is a resemblance of some kind between God's personhood and the human personhood with which the speaker will be familiar. Yet there cannot be a straightforward resemblance between God's personhood and human personhood. Much language about God includes predicates which, in mundane contexts would attribute properties to items that God Himself could not possess, since to do so would undermine His ontological transcendence.

The nature of many of the fundamental Divine characteristics cannot be separated, conceptually speaking from that of others. Hence the nature of Divine agency is bound up with the nature of Divine love, Divine personhood and other key Divine features. All these features are affected by 'otherness' in virtue of their interrelationships with Divine transcendence. 'God's transcendence means that God is not one instance among others of a general sort of thing, distinguished from (and ranked hierarchically with respect to) those others by the supreme degree to which it exhibits the designated quality' (Tanner, 2013, pp. 138–139).

In the case of a transcendent deity, there are some divine properties that humans cannot fully know about or understand and some divine properties which, in principle, no other item could possess, even to a lesser degree. Yet the religious believer often employs a range of predicates in whose standard use properties are attributed to items other than the Divine. It might be objected here that in the case of a fundamental claim such as 'God is a person', there must be *some* aspects of the Divine nature that other entities can share, in virtue of which this claim is true. So, even if God's personhood is 'beyond' human personhood in ways that cannot be fathomed by human thinkers, there must be some 'resemblance' between His nature and human nature on which the appropriateness of 'God is a person' is founded.

However, matters are not straightforward in the way this objection assumes, and the problems again stem from transcendence itself. There must be profound links between divine personhood properties and many other divine properties in virtue of which God is epistemologically and ontologically transcendent. Hence, even those divine properties which the believer would claim to know something about, understand something of – properties which apparently in principle other items can share, such as aspects of the divine nature in virtue of which God is a person, differ to an extent (and to what extent it seems that the believer cannot know) from those properties anything else would possess in virtue of being a person. Despite this fact, the believer employs predicates primarily ascribable to secular objects in order to attribute properties to God.

Consider, by way of contrast, the predicate ' – is a bank'. This has (at least) two meanings. At least two distinct properties may be attributed to things in uses of this predicate – the property of being a financial institution and the property of being the side of a river. Needless to say, there is no relation between the two meanings or the two properties involved. On the other hand, from the perspective of the believer there must be a deep affinity between the property attributed to, say Jones with ' – is a person' and the property attributed to God with ' – is a person'.

The proposal I now defend and explain is that the relationship between 'God is a person' and 'Jones is a person' has an illuminating parallel in the form of how 'The question is hard' relates to 'The chair is hard.' In the latter pair of sentences, we do not have a case of simple ambiguity as in ' – is a bank'. Now the property attributed to the chair is not the same property as the property attributed to the question. What is involved in the chair's hardness includes being resistant to the touch, uncomfortable for sitting on and improved by cushions. A question cannot have this property. Hence a question cannot be harder, or less hard, than a chair.

Yet, there clearly is a close relationship of some kind between the property possessed by the question and the property possessed by the chair. Now it seems reasonable to me to describe ' – is hard' when ascribed to a question as a metaphorical extension of ' – is hard' when ascribed to physical objects; admittedly the metaphor is old and tired. What account of ' – is hard' as applied to questions can explain what goes on in such metaphorical extension? Is it in any way applicable to the central instances of religious language such as 'God is a person'?

Aquinas rejected the view that the central cases of religious language such as 'God is a person' were metaphorical, on the ground that if X is metaphorically P, then it is not really P at all. It was for this reason that he insisted that the analogical – his characterization of much religious language – was a branch of the literal (Aquinas, 1964, Question 13).

A believer might be half inclined to accept that 'God is a person' is literally false but that what can be expressed by using this sentence is the best that humans can achieve when trying to capture a central feature of their God, given their limited knowledge and understanding of him. On the other hand, some may want to resist even the slightest suggestion that there is *any* sense in which 'God is a person' is false. They will assert that it is, after all, one of the most important statements that they wish to make about God. Their view could be that, though God may elude human knowledge and understanding to a degree, nevertheless God is 'at least' what humans think he is rather than merely different from what humans think he is. Hence, from this perspective, 'God is a person' is not so much false as insufficient.

A similar little debate can be held over many non-religious examples of metaphor – for example, those used to describe features of personality. Consider 'Alice has a sharp tongue.' On the one hand, it may be felt that this is literally false, since there is nothing sharp about Alice's tongue. For instance, it would not cut paper. On the other hand, it may equally be claimed that we can be saying something significant and 'true' about Alice here. The sense metaphorically expressed by 'Alice has a sharp tongue' is, at least in part, the thought that she is good at saying nasty things. And if it is true that she is good at saying nasty things, there is nothing half-baked about this truth; it is not, because metaphorically expressed, a watered down kind of truth. What is metaphorical is not the truth but the way it is expressed.

At first sight, the same kind of analysis of 'God is a person' is less convincing, but I hope to show that, in the end, it admits of a similar treatment. If 'God is a person' can metaphorically express a sense, that sense or proposition can have a truth value in as full a fashion as literally expressed claims.

Do I stumble at the first fence? For it has to be admitted that some cases of metaphorical claims about God do not obviously help my case. For instance, 'God is a rock' expresses its sense metaphorically, and we certainly would want to say – 'All the same, God is not *really* a rock.' Nevertheless, when we say the latter, we are not retracting what might be expressed by the first utterance. We are ruling out something that the first utterance might have expressed, had it been doing its expressing literally and not metaphorically – that God is physically a rock – of granite constitution, perhaps.

Now, it might be thought that a consequence of saying that 'God is a person' expresses its sense metaphorically ought to be, following the 'rock' case, that we can go on to say: 'But God is not really a person.' Yet this would, of course, seriously worry many religious believers. They really do want to say that God is a person. The only acceptable way of construing a *denial* that God is a person echoing a denial that God is literally speaking a rock is that the denial rules out the kind of personhood that might be attributed to a human being in a literal application of 'is a person'.

Suppose for a moment what I am denying – that 'God is a person' expresses its sense literally when uttered by a believer in an appropriate religious context. If this were so, there would seem to be no reason why we should not treat the ascription of the predicate ' – is a person' in the divine context as being similar to the ascription of that same predicate in, say, 'Jones is a person.' Hence, the kind of personhood being attributed to God would at least involve the same property – that of being a person, as that attributed to Jones. Yet I have argued that, whatever it is about God that makes 'God is a person' true differs radically from whatever it is about Jones that makes 'Jones is a person' true. This strongly suggests, then, that 'God is a person' cannot express its sense literally in the characteristic religious context of utterance. We do not, however, have a knock down argument here for the claim that it expresses its sense metaphorically instead. One of the obstacles in the way of producing such an argument is the familiar issue to which I have already referred – the contested nature of the distinction between the literal and the metaphorical and that the latter category appears to include a variety of language uses. All I can do here is to explore the plausibility of suggesting that it expresses its sense metaphorically, by showing how it compares with other examples which clearly do involve metaphorical expression.

It may well be thought that not nearly enough has been said to deal with the justifiable unease that is provoked by characterizing key uses of religious language as metaphorical. There surely *is* a crucial sense in which under no circumstances should 'God is a person' be linked with the thought that He is not *really* a person. I want to explore this issue further by exploring the phenomenon of 'irreducible metaphor' noted by Alston (1964). He cites cases of language about mental states such as 'the stabbing pain' and 'she feels depressed.' He talks of metaphors that 'cannot die' (p. 100). In addition Searle (1979), mentions spatial language that is used about time. He offers a couple of examples: 'Time flies' and 'The hours crawled by' (p. 109). We can add others, such as 'I don't want to cut my stay short' and 'I have been here a long time.'

An interesting feature of these examples is that it is counter-intuitive to follow them up with a remark of the form: 'But X is not really P.' Suppose we followed a claim that 'I have a stabbing pain' expresses its sense metaphorically with the observation: 'But the pain is not really stabbing.' The denial could be intended to rule out a possible sense that the sentence might have expressed literally, to the effect that a pain could really stab you, say, in the leg, as could a knife or a dagger, cutting the skin and drawing blood. Yet, at the same time, such a denial is admittedly difficult to take seriously, since we do wish to maintain, actually, that the pain really is a stabbing pain. Again, consider the assertion that 'The hours crawled by' expresses its sense metaphorically, and imagine that we proceeded to 'explain' our metaphor verdict by asserting that the hours did not really crawl by. That denial could be an attempt to exclude a possible sense that the first sentence might express literally, to the effect that the hours truly crawled, as might crocodiles or babies. And again, we may well feel a reluctance to proceed with the denial, in view of our concern to maintain that the hours really did crawl by. It seems characteristic of at least some irreducible metaphor of the form 'S is P' that the implied denial 'But S is not really P' 'feels' wrong.

When a metaphor is 'irreducible', what are the implications? Suppose 'Jones spoke sharply' metaphorically expresses the thought that Jones said something crossly. We can also use a sentence such as 'Jones said something crossly' to say something similar to what might be metaphorically expressed by 'Jones spoke sharply.' Yet, although we may succeed in saying something 'similar', we have not said exactly the same thing. For what we are compelled to call the sharp and cutting character of Jones's comment has somehow been omitted. What has been left out is a resemblance of some kind between Jones' remark and the physical character of something sharp, such as a knife. If we attempt to capture this resemblance, we will be compelled to use further metaphor, such as 'Jones's remark cut Susan to the quick'; 'Jones spoke in such a way as to wound Susan' and so on.

Why, if 'God is a person' expresses its sense metaphorically, must the metaphor be irreducible? To see this, I will need to develop a *reductio ad absurdam* argument. Take our case – 'God is a person' and imagine that it can metaphorically express something. Now, suppose for the sake of *reductio*, that it is *also* possible to express that something literally in an utterance of a distinct sentence 'God is Q.' Since the latter is literally expressed, we have no reason to think that whatever property 'is Q' attributes to God differs radically from the feature that could be assigned to Jones in a sentence such as 'Jones is Q.' Yet this cannot be: God's transcendence means that His personhood differs radically from the personhood that Jones can possess. Hence, the very possibility of a literal paraphrase of 'God is a person' is ruled out. Any alternative mode of presenting matters will involve just as much metaphorical expression as the original 'God is a person'. It is characteristic of irreducible metaphor that any attempt at alternative modes of expressing whatever sense is concerned also involves further metaphorical expression.

That there are irreducible metaphors does not breach Searle's 'Principle of Expressibility' (1969): 'Whatever can be meant can be said' (Searle, 1969, p. 20). This holds unless Searle were to claim that using irreducible metaphor for some reason does not really count as 'saying'. It is hard to imagine how that contention might be justified.

Comparison, metaphor and transcendence discourse

I now want to defend the thesis that at least some of the central assertions of religious discourse about a transcendent God involve comparison metaphors. To do so, I need to explain what comparison metaphors are supposed to be and to examine some objections to the idea. I will not assume that all metaphor involves comparison: I suggest that discussions of metaphor often suffer from the implicit assumption that there is just one kind of phenomenon called metaphor; in my view, there are quite a variety of semantic phenomena at issue here.

Aristotle is the classical source of comparison theory. He examines the question of metaphor in his 'Rhetorica' and 'De Poetica'. Whilst approving strongly of metaphor, he clearly thought of it as linguistic decoration that could serve to make language more vivid. Aristotle felt that metaphor consists in giving something a name that belongs to something else and that this essentially involves comparison. He believed that similes are metaphors. For example, when the poet says of Achilles that he 'leapt on the foe as a lion', this is simile. When he says of him 'The lion leapt', it is a metaphor. Here, since both are courageous, he has transferred to Achilles the name of 'lion'.

Aristotle has been alleged by some to hold a form of 'object comparison' theory of metaphor. According to such a theory, metaphor speaks of one object instead of another to trigger a comparison between the two. Thus Achilles is referred to as a lion, implying that Achilles and the lion resemble each other in one or more respects. The comparison theory in this form is open to the obvious objection that the item selected and suggested for comparison may not exist. For instance, one might say of a mean professional colleague at Christmas: 'Scrooge has gone into his room'. The objection depends on the thought that it would be nonsense to say that a real existent resembled something which did not exist, in such and such respects, since objects which do not exist cannot have properties. I shall assume that this thought is right. (To anyone who wanted to argue that non-existent objects can have properties, I would simply say that I would rather avoid the issue, especially as a more plausible version of a comparison theory which I support does not involve the comparison of 'objects' at all.)

Aristotle's account of simple metaphors involving comparisons – those which can, in his view, just as easily be expressed in similes, suggest that such metaphors can be 'paraphrased' by literal alternatives. That is to say, in terms of the conceptual framework employed in the last section, the sense expressed metaphorically by a certain utterance can also be expressed literally by a distinct utterance.

A more plausible version of the comparison theory, but still in the Aristotelian tradition, is that properties rather than objects are compared. A property of Achilles, for example, is implied by the metaphor to be like a property of a lion. By 'property' is meant 'universal', as opposed to actual instances of properties ('tropes') – the universal redness rather than the redness of the pillar box near the police station in the centre of Sheffield – the universal courage rather than the courage exhibited by Achilles on a particular occasion. Such a theory enables us, say, to speak of the property of being a dragon as being more like the property of being a lizard than it is like the property of being a horse, and other things of this kind. There do not have to be such things as real dragons for a property comparison account of a metaphor such as 'Mrs Jones is a dragon' to be intelligible. On such an account, certain universals exemplified by Mrs Jones are said, by means of an utterance of this sentence, to resemble certain universals associated with dragons.

The 'property comparison' version of a comparison theory of metaphor escapes another objection levelled by Searle against such theories. He objects that even if the object with which the comparison is made does exist, it may not possess the appropriate property. Consider 'Richard is a gorilla'. This, on the comparison view, compares properties of Richard with properties of a gorilla; if sufficient resemblances obtain between the properties, then an utterance of the sentence in question may express a sense or proposition that is true. In most contexts, it is clear that the properties of gorillas being put forward for comparison would be such as fierceness, nastiness and proneness to violence. 'But suppose ethological investigation shows … that gorillas are not at all fierce and nasty' (Searle, 1979, p. 102).

My response to this is that since it is universals that are being compared, and not instances of properties, it would not matter in the least if gorillas turned out not to have those properties that most people at present believe them to have. The presence of the term 'gorilla' may be regarded simply as an aid to the identification of which universal(s) are being referred to; it can perform this role even if gorillas turn out not to have those characteristics that most people at present believe them to have. Of course, once the gentle nature of gorillas became common knowledge, then, over the long term at least, it would become impossible to use a token of 'Richard is a gorilla' to express metaphorically the sense it could easily express at present.

It is argued by Searle and others that it must be incorrect to construe all metaphors as comparisons, for in some cases there is no such similarity as a comparison should reveal. Now I do not want to say, as, indeed I remarked earlier, that every case of what might reasonably be called metaphor involves comparison. Nonetheless, since the examples Searle uses in his attempt to refute comparison theories are those very examples of metaphor that I am claiming to be closest to sentences of religious language such as 'God is a person.' I will dwell for a while on his comments.

Searle would deny, for example, a similarity between coldness and being unemotional to support 'Alice is cold' metaphorically conveying that Alice is unemotional. In 'Time flies' or 'The hours crawled by', there is nothing, according to him, that time does and the hours do that actually resembles flying or crawling. Instead, he thinks that metaphors of this kind are based on mere psychological association – contingent facts about our sensibilities, whether culturally or naturally determined.

The plausibility of his contentions here rests upon the fact that some examples rather like the ones he gives quite clearly do rest upon 'facts about our sensibilities'. There is no similarity, for example, between sad music and a sad person. We can sometimes say, (perhaps) metaphorically, that the music is sad because, as a result of our contingent sensibilities, the music makes us feel sad. However, surely Searle is incorrect about at least some of the examples of metaphors about mental states, abstract objects and time. There is a similarity *of a kind* between hardness – the property of a chair (for instance) and hardness – the property of a question; a similarity between the property of being hot or fiery and the property of being prone to sudden fits of temper ('hot tempered', etc.). Searle's dismissal of a comparison account strikes me as especially implausible for those cases where terms are transferred from one sensory modality to another. Consider, for instance – 'A sharp sound' (touch to sound), 'A rough sound' (the same) and 'harmonious colours' (sound to sight).

But again, the issue is confused, and Searle's line made to seem more convincing than it should by the presence even in this area of some instances which do seem to fit what he says. It may well be thought, for instance, that a 'loud colour' is not a colour which possesses a non-relational property which resembles some non-relational property that a sound might possess. To continue this story, the situation is rather that as a result of our contingent sensibilities, certain colours and certain sounds cause us to notice them particularly. Loud sounds stand out for us, hence we call certain colours that we notice more than others 'loud'. (Admittedly, this may not be the full story – there is also a suggestion of vulgarity in 'loud colour'.)

Searle's argument that in none of these cases can the metaphor be based on any kind of similarities is simply that the similarities cannot be stated. ' … the bald assertion of similarity, with no specification of the respect of similarity, is without content' (Searle, 1979, p. 109). His remarks seem to me to ignore the possibility that there may be genuine similarities which are such that they cannot be said to obtain by means of any utterance expressing something literally. Searle assumes that a 'literal similarity' must be capable of literal expression. This could be a substantial thesis. If so, we are entitled to ask him how he knows it to be true – he has not shown it. He might make it a matter of definition that a literal similarity was capable of literal expression. We could then ask him why there should not also be similarities that are not literal in his sense. What, if any grounds could there be for the claim that such similarities would not be 'genuine' similarities? There might be different reasons why different brands of similarities could not be specified literally.

Why we should be unable, for example, to explain in literal terms what the similarity is between the hardness of a question and the hardness of a chair is difficult to say. But is the onus on us to explain, failing which any claimed similarity can be denied? After all, we can provide an explanation of the similarity of a kind – that the question makes us feel uncomfortable – it resists solution – hard objects also can make us feel uncomfortable – they are resistant to the touch. Yet our 'explanation' still seems to be couched in metaphorical form. Indeed, I think that the 'hard question' is an example of irreducible metaphor, and any attempt to describe the similarity between the hardness of the question and the hardness of objects will also involve metaphorical expression. Yet does any of this suggest that there cannot be a similarity? I cannot see that it does.

In the case of religious language, of course, a believer may explain that God's ontological transcendence prevents many of his aspects from being specified literally. For the possibility of literal specification seems to entail the possibility that God has the same property that something else also could possess, at least in principle. And there are divine properties of which this is not true.

Let me summarize now the version of the property comparison theory which I think is appropriate for, say 'Man is a wolf', and for many other similar examples and state how the theory might work for religious statements. The comparison theory does not pretend to provide a comprehensive explanation of how given sentence types with such and such meanings are capable of such and such metaphorical expression of such and such senses. It claims rather to give a basic sketch of what it is that the utterance expresses metaphorically. 'Man is a wolf' can metaphorically express the following: certain universals exemplified in man resemble certain universals thought to be exemplified by wolves. Like Olscamp (1970), I want to say that whether what is expressed is true is settled one way or the other by whether enough of the claimed resemblances obtain. 'The truth of the metaphor is discovered by determining whether there is a real correspondence between the properties compared' (Olscamp, 1970, p. 82). Whatever is expressed by many of the utterances that employ comparison metaphor could equally well be expressed literally by an utterance of a distinct sentence; in such an explicit literal formulation, the respective universals would be identified and the respects in which the resemblances were supposed to hold would be spelled out.

Also, there are irreducible comparison metaphors. These can still be used to make claims to the effect that similarities obtain between certain universals. 'The question is hard' can say that certain universals exemplified by this question resemble in some respects universals believed to be exemplified by physically hard things. 'Time flies' can say that our perception of the passing of time exemplifies certain universals, which resemble in certain respects universals believed to be exemplified by flying objects, etc. Alternative means of expression of the nature of the similarities are available, but these will still be metaphorical.

Searle (1979, p. 106) objects to comparison theories because, in his view they are too vague. Resemblance or similarity must be in some respect(s), but anything can be said to resemble anything in some respect. 'Inasmuch as similarity is a vacuous predicate we need to be told in what respect two things are similar for the statement that they are similar to have informative content.'

Now, I defend comparison theory to support the point that the obtaining of resemblances is part of the truth condition of at least *some* assertions that are expressed metaphorically. This is, in some sense, a rather general and 'vague' thesis. If Searle is suggesting that if we take the sentence type 'Man is a wolf', then the standard meanings of its words are not alone sufficient for fixing what it may metaphorically express, he is right, but would not be right to complain about it. The sentence taken by itself fails to indicate in what respects the similarity is supposed to hold. Nevertheless, anyone able to use and understand the sentence, having an adequate grasp of the semantic rules for the use of 'man', 'wolf, together with a background of knowledge and culture essential to the language user, will be pointed by the meaning of the sentence type in the right direction.

In addition – the full detail of the context of utterance, including the speaker's and hearer's shared beliefs about mankind and their previous conversation, will finally bring into focus the respects in which the comparison is being made. I said that the context 'brings into focus' the respects in which the resemblances are being asserted. Yet it is true that in many cases, at least, no very exact range of resemblances has to obtain for the metaphorical expression to succeed. I agree with Black (1979) that metaphors, like much other language, are not intended to be absolutely precise. But this does not mean that they do not have truth conditions. If insufficient resemblances obtain, then that which is metaphorically expressed is not true.

'God is a person' can say, metaphorically, that certain universals held to be exemplified by God resemble in certain respects universals believed to be exemplified by humans who are persons. No literal expression of the resemblances is possible. That the resemblances obtain is, on the view I am defending, part of what such a sentence could metaphorically express.

Again, someone like Searle might be inclined to complain that this proposal is vague. The only response to this is that we have to rely upon the context of the utterance of a sentence such as 'God is a person' to ensure that a reasonably precise sense is expressed. That context is likely to consist of a community of religious believers, who worship together. Each of them takes it that their fellow members are directing worship to the same unsurpassable being as the object of their own worship. Each will be aware of at least some of their fellows' beliefs about God. Some of these beliefs may not be entirely comprehensible. Perhaps the community in question has some kind of shared religious experience. All these contextual features serve to constrain the possible senses that 'God is a person' might express. Were we able to be entirely explicit and precise about how this happens, we would almost have given a specification of the sense itself. However, it has been argued that no literal specification is possible. Hence we will have to rest content with our general reflections here on the influence of context.

Searle argues that the idea of comparison may be involved in the process of comprehending metaphor but is not, as he puts it, part of the meaning of metaphor. He holds that the existence of similarity is not part of the truth condition of whatever is expressed metaphorically by a given utterance. Since I have already rejected in the foregoing discussion much of Searle's criticism of comparison theory, I do not feel obliged, as he does, to abandon comparison theory.

Furthermore, attempts to talk of the transcendent are not consistent with Searle (1979). He insists that a theory of metaphor 'must explain how it is possible to utter "S is P" and both mean and communicate that S is R' (p. 98). Searle details his overall explanation in a complex and sophisticated way at the end of his paper. He holds that using 'is P' calls to mind the meaning, and hence, truth condition, associated with '– is R' in the special ways that metaphorical utterances have of calling other things to mind, and he specifies some of these ways. Reverting now to our example of 'God is a person', a Searlian view of it would be roughly as follows. The believer says 'God is a person', meaning 'God is X', where 'person' plainly does not mean the same as 'X', but somehow 'God is a person' calls to mind the meaning and hence truth conditions associated with something being X. Now the meaning and truth conditions associated with ' – is X' are available to the believer, if at all, via metaphorical language once again. We saw earlier that language about God, if metaphorical because of his ontological transcendence, must be irreducibly metaphorical. Otherwise his ontological transcendence is ultimately infringed. And now, on the Searle view, the believer will have the same problem in understanding 'God is X' as he had in understanding 'God is a person', and a vicious infinite regress threatens to ensue; vicious since before the believer can understand one piece of irreducibly metaphorical language about God, he must understand an infinite number of other pieces of irreducibly metaphorical language.

Davidson (1980), argues that there is no special metaphorical dimension of meaning but that metaphors are sentences with an ordinary literal meaning which have certain effects: 'Metaphor makes us see one thing as another by making some literal statement that inspires or prompts the insight' (p. 253). '...what we attempt in 'paraphrasing' a metaphor cannot be to give its meaning, for that lies on the surface: rather, we attempt to evoke what the metaphor brings to our attention' (p. 252).

I agree with Davidson that expression types and sentence types do not have anything other than their ordinary meaning when figuring in an utterance which expresses a sense metaphorically. But in my view, it is the combination of the words in their standard meaning with the context of the utterance that enables the sense to get expressed metaphorically. As against Davidson, I would want to deny that any literal expression of a sense occurs in the course of an utterance which expresses a sense metaphorically. Davidson's idea would be, presumably, that in say 'Man is a wolf' we have a sense literally expressed to the effect that Man is a wolf, and that though this is false, it evokes certain effects in the hearer. But surely, no such sense is expressed. Indeed, it is difficult to imagine what such a sense would be if it were expressed – it would be nearer incoherence than falsity. And other more interesting metaphors would provide intractable problems for Davidson's claim that a sense is literally expressed: 'But I will wear my heart upon my sleeve For doves to peck at' (Othello).

It is arguable that a perfectly clear and coherent sense gets expressed metaphorically here. But if we asked Davidson to provide us with a literally expressed sense which has such and such effects, I suspect that he would be utterly at a loss.

To conclude this discussion of transcendence language, let us take stock. I have defended the claim that aspects of transcendence can be captured by employing irreducible comparison metaphor. I have done this by showing that comparison metaphor appears to achieve similar feats in other contexts. I attribute a different property to a sound with 'It was a sharp sound' from the property I attribute to a knife with 'It was a sharp knife.' In doing this, it was argued, I express a sense to the effect that certain similarities obtain between the universal sharpness, exemplified by, say knives, and certain universals exemplified by the sound in question. Context of utterance plays an important role in determining what these similarities are supposed to be. If comparison metaphor can be employed to speak of a transcendent God, then, we saw, this metaphor may well have to be irreducible.

I have highlighted the inevitable presence of irreducible metaphor in transcendence language because of the important implications for the stand-off between religious exclusivisms and religious pluralisms. Phrases that when understood literally may appear to be in tension with each other can sometimes be reconciled when construed in some kind of metaphorical fashion. Frequently, literal construals of phrases employed metaphorically imply impossible things about the categories to which things belong. 'He is a rock' is not literally compatible with 'He really takes in what people say to him' because rocks are not the kind of item that can physically 'take in' anything. 'Jane is a blunt speaker. She makes penetrating comments' when taken literally imply that speech can be both sharp and blunt in the way a knife might be. 'When Jones is under pressure, the volume of his publications increases' and 'She spoke up and shouted him down' also, if understood literally, involve incoherence and categorical confusion.

Consider the classic example of the clash between Christianity and both Judaism and Islam over Trinitarian and incarnational doctrine. The devout Christian will hold that Christ is the Son of God, and that this, of course excludes how Islam conceives of Allah. For Islam, the very idea of incarnation detracts from His absolute transcendence and simplicity. There can be few more obvious instances of incompatible religious doctrines. Yet all Christians know that Jesus is not *literally* the Son of God. Such a claim may, of course provoke fierce denunciation, since it sounds only too much like a direct denial of what is at the heart of Christianity. The denial of literal sonship covers, in particular, the obvious facts that God was not and is not a human father and that even if a Christian wanted to elaborate the notion of fatherhood by speculating that sperm that did not originate from a human male was introduced into Mary somehow, this sperm could not be part of the normal processes of human biology. Moreover, its not originating from a human male would hardly contribute much to a positive claim that God is Jesus's father. The denial also incorporates the self-evident point that fathers and sons as humans understand them are separate people. A human son is not and cannot be 'one' with his father if anything like numerical identity is meant here.

Theologians have attempted for centuries to develop a coherent and convincing account of the Doctrine of the Trinity, of which Christ being the Son of God is one element. They have never succeeded (Tuggy, 2003) and arguably never will. Part of the explanation for this may relate to their attempts to provide a literal abstract characterization of something that admits, at best, of an account riddled with irreducible metaphor.

Yet a denial of the literal truth is *not* the same as a denial of a profound truth. The language here works at a deep level, yet not literally. We saw above that not all claims made with metaphorical language are half-hearted. Islam's rejection of the Christian claim interpreted literally embodies an assumption that the language of that claim should be taken literally. As such, of course Islam rejects it.

Comparing religious claims and holism

Quine, Davidson and others have made us familiar with holist perspectives on meaning and belief. For instance, Davidson (2001) remarks:

> ... it is impossible to make sense of the idea of having only one or two beliefs. Beliefs do not come one at a time: what identifies a belief and makes it the belief that it is the relationship (among other things) to other beliefs ... because of the fact that beliefs are individuated and identified by their relations to other beliefs, one must have a large number of beliefs if one is to have any. Beliefs support one another, and give each other content ... (p. 124)

Obvious instances of holism can be found in science. In Newtonian mechanics, for example, the meaning of each of the ideas of force, mass and acceleration cannot be wholly separated from the meanings of the others. Within a set of concepts, beliefs and doctrines associated with a particular faith, we should also expect to find holistic characteristics. For example, consider the concept of personhood as applied to God within Christianity. Its meaning is bound up with its interrelationships with other concepts also applied to God within this faith, such as goodness, knowledge, power to act intentionally, unsurpassable abilities, forgiveness and fatherhood. The point relates to the so-called 'hermeneutical circle', according to which we sometimes cannot comprehend the character of the parts without appreciating the nature of the 'whole' of which they are part. Having moved to the whole, we cannot properly understand it without grasping the nature of the parts.

We cannot limit the interconnections that prevail between concepts. Accordingly, for instance, we cannot regard ideas within Christianity as in a kind of conceptual ghetto, with no links to ideas outside religion or no links to ideas in other religions. Nevertheless, the connections between ideas *within* Christianity will be particularly salient for their very identity. Now, suppose we wanted to compare the Hindu's claim that the ultimate Reality is 'the blissful, universal consciousness of Brahman' with the Christian thought that this Reality is personal (Hick, 2004).

A commentator disposed to religious pluralism might want to say that the Christian and the Hindu are talking about the same reality. There is, of course a prima facie conflict between the Hindu and the Christian characterization of the ultimate Reality. Yet, if we fully appreciate holist considerations here, we realize that these characterizations cannot be directly compared. To suppose that they could, would be to imagine that these descriptions can be abstracted away from their sets of interrelationships with other ideas within each of the faiths concerned, that a stand-alone meaning could be identified for each description and hence that they could be compared directly. These suppositions are recognisably incoherent once we grasp the crucial implications of holism about ideas and concepts.

Hence, holist considerations afford an additional motive for rejecting religious exclusivism. Exclusivists who are very concerned about conflicts between specific claims within their faiths and 'corresponding' claims in other faiths may fail to appreciate holist considerations. They may be in possession of an over-simple vision of the possibility of comparing and contrasting central claims made by different World Faiths. At the same time, it must be conceded to Barnes that there are still some apparent conflicts to which a holist perspective is inapplicable. Where, for instance one faith holds that there is a God or some Ultimate Reality, but another (a variety of Buddhism, for instance) denies this, the fundamental incompatibility between the two beliefs is undeniably real.

Pluralism and approaches to religious education

Contrary to what commentators such as Barnes claim, the kind of pluralism I am advocating is perfectly compatible with taking religious differences seriously. To repeat, the position for which I have argued here should not be identified with any vague liberal idea that all religions are the 'same'. Now, if pupils are not committed to any particular faith, helping them to understand this point may not appear to be too much of a challenge. Perhaps from a kind of detached, Olympian standpoint, a student on the religious sidelines can appreciate this point without it troubling aspects of their identity. However, Barnes might urge, the situation is very different where pupils are strongly committed to a particular faith and adhere to their beliefs in an exclusivist fashion.

Good teaching always tries to begin where the pupils are. So a liberal-minded teacher who shared my modest pluralist sentiments would be making a grave mistake if she confronted an exclusivist pupil with an uncompromising[1] agenda. The aim should rather be to offer curriculum content and pedagogy that gently challenged pupils with existing exclusivist standpoints. It should seek to help students to realize for themselves that they can relinquish their exclusivism without threatening their religious beliefs and that a strong religious commitment is perfectly compatible with an openness to the possibility that there are other routes to the truth.

What kinds of approaches would be appropriate? Students need to realize that there are subjects and domains outside the religious sphere that may *also* be susceptible to a range of interpretations, where there may be at least the appearance of conflict, yet where it is plausible to insist that no one interpretation should be regarded as the last word on the situation. When we describe human situations this is often the case.

There was a family occasion years ago when I had the privilege of hearing four of my aunts talk about their childhood. You would be forgiven for thinking that they did not have the same parents, given the variety of narratives that were offered about the 'same' piece of history. Of course, different children bring out differences in parental behaviour, and a given child may have had experiences at home that her siblings missed. Yet such points could not explain all of the profound differences between one aunt's story and another.

When we hear about the break up of a marriage or are offered a verdict on the causes of a war, it is much the same. If there is conflict about 'facts' such as someone's date of birth, or which school was attended, then at least one of the claims is false. However, much else in the narratives is a matter of interpretation and open to more than one at that.

A possible way of modelling this situation might be those familiar ambiguous figures such as the duck/rabbit diagram, though here, of course, there are only two ways of seeing. The two ways 'conflict', but it would be absurd to rule that the duck verdict was 'correct', and hence this must mean that the rabbit verdict was 'wrong'.

It would be wrong, I think, to characterize what I am suggesting as a relativist account of verdicts on social phenomena. It is rather that many social situations by their very nature are open to a range of interpretations, some of which may seem to be in conflict with each other. To restrict interpretations to those that are consistent with each other or to rule out future interpretations that may not conform with those currently affirmed would be to deny the very nature of social phenomena or to distort them by insisting that they resemble the empirical states of affairs that the natural sciences seek to capture. In the latter case, descriptions that conflict – for instance, about the character of the planet Jupiter, point to the falsity of one or both of those descriptions. This does not always apply to accounts of social phenomena.

Another helpful analogy for students might be drawn from aesthetic verdicts on arts and performances. If aesthetic verdicts are more than mere feelings, then we can note that equally well-informed critics may reach conflicting verdicts on, say a painting, a musical composition or the performance of a play. It would be an unjustified distortion of the situation to insist that one or both of the critics 'must' be wrong in the case of conflict. The rich and complex character of art is, or so it may be argued, just the kind of phenomenon that is open to a range of interpretations.

However, this analogy will be ruled out as a non-starter by those who hold that aesthetic judgements are wholly subjective – that they merely express the feelings of the judges concerned. Needless to say, I cannot offer a conclusive defence of objective elements in some aesthetic judgements in my contribution to this book.

Neither the social nor the aesthetic analogies I have suggested are readily accessible by primary age children but would be better pursued at the secondary stage. Ideally, there would be teaching from more than one curriculum area. Literature, drama, history, performing arts, and others, could be involved.

Teaching in the pluralist spirit I am advocating should be a requirement both in common schools and in faith schools.

Note

1 I am grateful to Andrew Wright, who helped me to see the importance of this during some conversation and e-mail exchanges.

Afterword

J. Mark Halstead

This Afterword has two main purposes. The first is to follow up an issue which is touched on many times in both essays but which is not investigated systematically by either author. This is the question of the relationship between religious education and liberal values and the extent to which religious education has a responsibility in a liberal society to support and reinforce the aims of liberal education. The intention is not to take the debate in a different direction from the key question about the kind of religious education that should be taught in a liberal democratic society characterized by growing religious diversity; it is simply to return to the central topic with an enriched sense of the issues at stake. The second purpose is to engage rather more fully with some of the recurring concepts in the debate, including religious diversity, 'religionism', exclusivism, pluralism, truth, metaphor, tolerance and respect. The underlying intention is to clarify, and test the strength of, the two authors' arguments and to consider their potential impact on the future of religious education.

Liberal values and religious education

It is central to a liberal worldview that 'the most justifiable kind of society is an open, pluralist, democratic one where there is maximum toleration of diversity and a commitment to free critical debate as the most rational means of advancing the pursuit of truth in all its forms' (McLaughlin, 1984, p. 75 f). The language here resonates closely with the language in which the current debate has been conducted: pluralism, toleration, diversity, rationality and truth. As

Davis recognizes, part of Barnes' underlying concern in his essay is to raise some questions about the relationship between liberal values and those of religious education. The relationship is a two-way one. First, there is the much discussed question of what place there is for the promotion of religious values in a specifically liberal and increasingly secular society. But there is also a second question that is discussed more rarely – how far religious education should serve the purposes of liberal education in the liberal state and uphold liberal values. This question hovers in the background of the current debate, though it is not tackled head-on. A number of possible answers present themselves. First, religious education, as part of the basic compulsory curriculum of all schools in England, could be held responsible for upholding the liberal educational values that underpin the overall curriculum decision-making process. Second, religious education could stand apart from the dominant liberal ideology and provide some kind of prophetic voice engaged in an ongoing critique of liberal values and even subverting these at times. Third, religious education could be more selective, supporting some liberal values but rejecting others, though this would raise the question of how the selection should be made – whether on the basis of those values which liberalism and religions hold in common, or on the basis of those which are considered most important for the maintenance of national security or other political goals or according to some altogether different criteria.

Barnes appears to go along with the third of these positions, accepting apparently without question that it is the role of religious education to help the liberal state to achieve its social aims such as tolerance and community cohesion but showing only hesitant support for the liberal belief that the development of rational autonomy is a fundamental aim of education. He does not make explicit any systematic basis on which he accepts some liberal values and is more hesitant about others. He is certainly aware that contextualizing the book in a liberal state has moral, educational and religious consequences, and some of these are discussed or at least touched on in his essay.

First, the liberal state adopts an inclusive approach to diversity, though, as Barnes notes, it seeks to shape diversity 'for civic and moral purposes' (this volume, p. 13). This suggests that it defines the toleration of diversity in terms of the incorporation of minorities in pluralist political structures and the development of multicultural policies in society. The liberal recognition of religious diversity is linked to two core liberal values: respect for persons (according to which all individuals are to be treated as self-determining, of supreme worth and as ends in themselves) and religious freedom (according to which individuals are free to hold, change or renounce religious beliefs and to engage in religious practices). So far, I think Barnes would be prepared to accept the liberal approach.

Secondly, liberalism holds that religious beliefs cannot be shown to be objectively true. This is why, rather than being built into the liberal framework, religion is left as a matter of individual choice and why religious proselytizing is banned in publicly funded institutions like the common school. It is here that Barnes parts company somewhat with conventional liberal thinking. He argues that the reason for banning proselytization and abandoning confessional education in common schools is nothing to do with a principled requirement of religious neutrality on all matters but more to do with practical difficulties associated with religious diversity. He further argues that indoctrination (generally considered anathema in liberal education) need not be a matter of major concern, though it is not completely clear whether this is because there is nothing ultimately wrong with indoctrination; or because there is something wrong with it but religious education does not actually engage in indoctrination; or because it is very hard in practice to indoctrinate anyone in the current cultural climate. The main argument that Barnes proposes against indoctrination is not a liberal but a religious one – that commitment to God should result from the free choice of individuals; but the problem here is that, though this argument may be decisive for Protestant Christians, it is less appealing to other faiths.

Davis tends to stand back generally from any discussion about the relation between religious education and liberal values, merely commenting wryly that he is not concerned with 'any vague liberal idea that all religions are the "same"' (this volume, p. 109) and that he 'makes no assumptions about the appropriateness' of the view that 'a neutral state should be explicit in its refusal to favour any one religion' (p. 64). In spite of this rather flippant side-stepping of a central liberal value, however, it is clear that Davis takes the values of liberalism and liberal education seriously. The description of 'good teaching' in the final section of his essay depicts a 'liberal-minded teacher' using rationality rather than indoctrination to gradually wean a pupil away from an exclusivist approach to personal faith (p. 110). Even more significantly, he attempts to construct a theological argument on the basis of rational liberal moral values, arguing that it would be 'an ethical obscenity' (p. 66) for God to restrict salvation to any one faith, because many people may never have the chance to hear the teachings of that particular faith. By 'ethical obscenity', he presumably means that, like racism, such a belief contravenes the core liberal value of justice, and he goes on to argue that children should be taught as part of their religious education that the faith of those who seek to restrict salvation in this way is both harmful and intolerable. In other words, Davis is arguing that there are some occasions where religious education should teach liberal values in preference to the religious values that some (perhaps many) people hold.

But can a secular liberal society allow any place at all for the teaching of religion in the common school? This simple question raises a number of further issues: Is there any connection between religious pluralism and the sort of political pluralism that liberalism supports? Is there any connection between multicultural education and multi-faith approaches to religious education? Are the rights of groups to be understood in the same way as the rights of individuals (e.g. to engage in religious practices)? Is religious neutrality a *sine qua non* for a liberal society? If there is significant overlap between liberal and religious values, does that justify the use of religious education to promote those values? Are religious values and liberal values in fact broadly in harmony or at loggerheads on fundamental issues?

To answer questions such as these, we need to take a momentary step back and focus on the nature of liberal societies. There is not space here for more than a very brief sketch of a framework of liberal values, but hopefully enough can be said to show that the framework represents a coherent set of interlocking values rather than a *smorgasbord* from which one can choose at will.

Liberalism may be said to have its origin in the tension that exists between individual liberty (understood as freedom of action so long as no harm to others ensues and freedom from constraint in the pursuit of one's own needs and interests) and equality (understood as the equal right of all individuals to the same freedom without discrimination). With reference to religion, for example, individual liberty can be understood in terms of freedom *to* hold or reject any particular religious beliefs, values and practices and freedom *from* any invidious indoctrination into beliefs he or she does not wish to share; the principle of equal rights refers to the freedom of all other individuals to hold the same or different or no religious beliefs. The tension between individual liberty and equal rights in many areas of life can only be resolved on a liberal view by decisions that are based on logically consistent rational justifications. In other words, the decisions must not be arbitrary or inconsistent or fail to take account of relevant factors, must not accept dogma (whether based on authority or revelation) uncritically and must not drift into the sort of relativism which insists that cultures, for example, can be understood only from within and on their own terms. Space does not allow a more detailed examination here of the different ways in which these three core values (liberty, equality and rationality) can be understood within liberalism, but it is worth noting that the three combine in different ways to generate a richer framework of liberal values. Personal autonomy is linked in particular to freedom and rationality; impartiality and respect for persons to rationality and equality; and justice and social rules to all three core values.

This liberal framework of values has produced theories in a number of different domains, though the political domain has always been the central arena for liberal debate (Rawls, 1993). Democracy is seen by liberals as the most rational safeguard against tyranny and a way of guaranteeing the equal right of citizens to determine for themselves what is in their own best interests. Key liberal causes include human rights, free speech, opposition to censorship, racial equality, social and political pluralism and opposition to the enforcement of morality through the criminal law. Other theories dependent on the liberal framework of values include liberal legal theory (based on the maintenance of order in society through the protection of persons and property), liberal economic theory (based on the balance between the free market economy and welfare considerations), liberal moral theory (including both consequentialism and distributive justice) and liberal educational theory.

All the values typically associated with liberal education – including personal autonomy, critical openness, equality of opportunity, citizenship, children's rights, the autonomy of academic disciplines, the celebration of diversity, the avoidance of indoctrination and the refusal to side with any definitive conception of the good – are based on the three fundamental liberal values of freedom, equality and rationality. In particular, the development of the rational mind is at the very core of liberal education. In his essay, Barnes worries that liberal rationality might come across as emotionally empty and lacking a balanced sense of personhood, but liberalism does not have to be understood so narrowly. Indeed, it may be part of rational decision-making to pay attention to all relevant factors including, as appropriate, a person's emotions, needs, values, attitudes, preferences, desires, social context and cultural background. Rationality plays a central part in developing children's ability to be open-minded, to engage in critical thinking, to choose freely from alternatives and base decisions on good reasons and thus to become autonomous individuals. Equality of respect is also a key value in liberal education, not least because abuse and disrespect generate friction in society and hinder the autonomous flourishing of individuals. Equality of respect for those whose beliefs, values, practices and characteristics differ from one's own underpins liberal policies opposing discrimination on irrelevant grounds such as the race, gender, ethnicity, nationality, religion, social class or sexuality of the individual; it also underpins multicultural education, which is seen as a source of enrichment, helping to free children from inherited biases and helping them to develop imagination, curiosity, reflective skills, sensitivity to others, intellectual humility and positive responses to diversity.

No single conception of the good life is favoured in political liberalism, and a vast range of life-styles, beliefs, commitments, priorities, occupational roles and life-plans form a marketplace of ideas within the liberal framework. Religion is thus seen as a private and voluntary matter for the individual, with the practice of religion (so long as no harm results) being a moral right based on the liberal value of individual freedom. The liberal state is expected to show official neutrality in the face of diversity in religious matters and to respect the individual freedom of conscience, for to do otherwise would undermine the marketplace of ideas.

We are now in a position to return to the matter of the relationship between liberal values and religious education. From a liberal perspective, it is important (and completely legitimate) for religious education to encourage children to reflect on their own religious views and to make a free choice whether to accept any religious teachings or not. This justifies teaching children *about* different religious and non-religious worldviews, in a critically open way, to make their free autonomous choice a reality. It *might* be legitimate to start children's education off from within a particular religious framework, so that they are not being educated in some kind of cultural vacuum, as long as the ultimate goal is autonomous decision-making about religion. It is not legitimate for common schools (i.e. schools not belonging to a particular faith or denomination) to teach children that one particular worldview or set of religious beliefs is true, because to do so would undermine the religious neutrality of the state. This means that adopting an exclusivist, confessional kind of religious education (i.e. teaching children that one particular faith has an exclusive claim on truth) *and* adopting a pluralist perspective (i.e. teaching them that all faiths are equally true) are both unacceptable on a liberal view, because neither approach can be shown to be based on objective truth.

So should religious education be a vehicle for the teaching of liberal values like tolerance and community cohesion, which the liberal state wishes children to take on board? From a liberal perspective, this is problematic. If the RE teacher says, 'There are good religious reasons why you should accept the values of community cohesion', that would be illegitimate on a liberal view, because it would be requiring children to accept something because it is religious. On the other hand, if the RE teacher says, 'There are good social and political reasons why you should accept this value', that would be going outside the subject domain and teaching citizenship instead. Perhaps the most the RE teacher could say would be, 'This is a value you should think seriously about', but that might not be geared sufficiently towards the required outcome, which is commitment to the principle of community cohesion. From a religious perspective, on the other hand, teaching liberal values could never be more than part of the aim of religious education, which also involves the study of aspects of life where rationality may not be central (such as spirituality, spontaneity, ambiguity and wonder or non-rational moral virtues like altruism or non-rational doctrines like the ineffability of God).

If it is also the role of religious education to provide children with information about different religious beliefs, this may include teaching that some believers reject liberal values. Children may learn that for some believers it may be more important to be a good Christian than a good citizen, while others may believe that religious attachments are more important than political ones as a source of identity and community cohesion or that the Islamic *umma*, for example, is more important than the national or global community. As a source of information about religious beliefs, religious education can perhaps encourage comparisons between liberal and religious values and provide the critical distance needed to examine and evaluate the impact on religious minorities of the 'active, muscular liberalism' (to use Prime Minister David Cameron's words) underpinning contemporary policy. Husband and Alam, for example, note that for Muslims the hidden message of community cohesion policies seems to be, '*We want you to be more actively engaged as citizens, but we want you to be more like us*' (2011, p. 3), whereas the message of the Prevent (i.e. counter-terrorism) policies is '*You must know that we cannot fully trust you and that we must, in the name of national security, subject your communities to intensive and intrusive surveillance*' (2011, p. 4). From a Muslim perspective, these messages are undoubtedly worrying, and we need now to explore the relationship between religious education and discriminatory practices more fully.

Exclusivism, religious education, racism and 'religionism'

We are now in a position to focus more directly on the main lines of argument in the debate between Barnes and Davis. Barnes maintains that contemporary pluralist religious education is incapable of challenging negative reactions to diversity because it misrepresents religions and in particular because it does not pay adequate attention to the intractable nature of religious difference. Davis, on the other hand, argues for a 'modest' form of religious pluralism as a better basis for religious education than religious exclusivism, which he regards as unethical, indeed as the cause of much negative reaction to diversity. He justifies his support for pluralism by arguing that different faiths normally focus on the same notion of ultimate reality even though they have different ways of conceiving this and that conflicting truth claims about religion are often based on a failure to appreciate the metaphorical nature of religious language, which may be open to different interpretations anyway. The next three sections of this Afterword focus on the main stages of the argument. The present section focuses on Davis's claim that religious exclusivism is responsible for much religious intolerance. The next section examines Davis's arguments in support of 'modest' pluralism, particularly what he says about religious language and truth. A further section discusses the concepts and importance of tolerance and respect more fully, and this leads into a re-consideration of Barnes' case against pluralist religious education and particularly his claim that pluralist or multi-faith religious education is incapable of teaching tolerance and respect for diversity because it misrepresents religions and therefore does not itself demonstrate the respect it teaches.

Both authors are interested in the role of religious education in challenging negative responses to diversity, including intolerance, prejudice, discrimination, stereotyping, disrespect, resentment, community tension and injustice. Clearly, any kind of perceived difference can be the target of these negative responses, though the focus of this volume is largely limited to religious differences. Davis narrows the focus of attention further by restricting his contribution to a discussion of religion as a source of intolerance, and more particularly, the disrespect towards other faiths that may result from the belief that one's own faith has an exclusive claim to truth. Barnes, on the other hand, (rightly, in my view) spreads his net more widely, pointing out that 'bigotry and intolerance are not vices confined to those who are religious'. He argues that religious education potentially has a role in challenging discrimination on any grounds (including race, ethnicity, etc. as well as religion), whether or not the discrimination is linked to the religious beliefs of the perpetrator.

Davis produces no compelling evidence to support the view either (a) that holding exclusivist religious beliefs necessarily results in prejudice and discrimination towards other faiths or (b) that prejudice and discrimination against particular religious faiths necessarily results from religious exclusivism. Jehovah's Witnesses, for example, and members of the Church of Jesus Christ of Latter-Day Saints are probably among the best known exclusivist faiths in the UK, but neither group is seriously criticized for disrespecting other faiths or generating community strife. Among non-Christian faith groups, Muslims are perhaps most likely to have a reputation for intolerance of other faiths, fanned mainly by the media's tendency to focus attention on a few Muslim extremists. However, many Muslim parents in England send their children to Christian schools, whether Anglican or Catholic, in preference to community schools. The reason given by Muslim parents for this preference is that the supposed religious neutrality of community schools often masks a secular approach, whereas Muslim parents typically prefer their children to be educated in an environment that respects religion and takes religious morality seriously (whatever the religion is) rather than in a secular environment (Halstead, 2005, p. 122). Many Muslims in England have the sense that they are on the same side as Christians in their resistance to the dominant secular values.

Probably the worst form of religious intolerance that is widespread in England today is Islamophobia (Parker-Jenkins et al., 2014, pp. 69–75), a neologism that refers to irrational, unjustified or excessive fear or hatred of Islam and of Muslims. Its more obvious manifestations include negative attitudes (intolerance and prejudice); negative actions (discrimination, harassment, social and economic exclusion); verbal and physical abuse and hate crimes against Muslims and their places of worship; and the vilification of Islam as a religion and a way of life. It may also refer to the negative stereotyping of Muslims as extremist, barbaric, treacherous, violent, uncivilized and sexist and to assumptions about the inferiority of Islamic culture and values (cf. Allen, 2010; Esposito and Kalin, 2011). It is true that Islamophobic activities are sometimes orchestrated by fundamentalist Christians, as in the well-publicized case of the Rev. Terry Jones, who burned a copy of the Qur'an at his church in Florida in 2011 following a bizarre attempt to justify his actions by putting the Holy Book on trial and finding it guilty of crimes meriting execution and burning. More often than not, however, hostility towards Islam has nothing to do with the attitude of other faiths to Islam but has its roots in perceptions of a political and economic threat or simply in gut feelings of suspicion, fear and hatred towards a visibly different group (since Muslims living in the UK tend to retain more external symbols of difference than most other groups, including food, clothing, personal appearance, lifestyle, festivals, language, places of worship and ties with the Middle East).

Even if we accept that the root causes of prejudice against religious minorities are more likely to be political and economic than religious, however, religion may still play a part sometimes as a rallying point and as a way of rationalizing the intolerance, though some have stressed a more direct link between religious exclusivism and religious bigotry and intolerance. John Hull in particular has written extensively about the arrogance and intolerance of those who believe in the exclusive truth of their own faith and who foster a sense of identity and solidarity by promoting negative attitudes towards other religions. Hull (2000, p. 76) calls this phenomenon 'religionism' because he sees a close parallel with racism, and he explains it as follows:

> We are better than they. We are orthodox; they are infidels. We are believers; they are unbelievers. We are right; they are wrong. The other is identified as the pagan, the heathen, the alien, the stranger, the invader, the one who threatens us and our way of life, and in contrast to whom we know what we are.

But like racism, religionism is more than a matter of individual prejudice. It may exist in institutional structures as well and have deep historical roots. It may also provide support for attitudes of intolerance that originate elsewhere. It may have catastrophic consequences in terms of war and conflict as well as injustice at an individual level. Hull's answer is to create an 'anti-religionist' education (following the model of anti-racist or anti-sexist education), which involves, first, using religious education to deconstruct the intolerant elements that have grown up within religious institutions as well as in individual believers and, second, reconstructing a syllabus that focuses on 'the religious experience of men and women in a global perspective' (2000, p. 82). Religious education should thus encourage students to reflect on how human beings should respond to 'that to which the spirituality of all religions bears witness' (2000, p. 82).

Davis seems to be partly under Hull's influence, at least insofar as he links the problem of religious intolerance to religious exclusivism and sees the solution to lie in a more pluralist approach to religious education. But there is a danger that Hull's approach may inadvertently fall into the trap of demonstrating the very arrogance and intolerance that he criticizes in others, especially when he wants to use religious education to change the self-identity and self-understanding of different religious communities so that they see other faiths as complementary to their own rather than in conflict with them. To clarify this point, we need to look more closely at the parallel Hull draws between racism and 'religionism'.

The initial parallel is clear enough. Just as there are racist beliefs (that one's own race is superior to others), racist attitudes (prejudice, intolerance and hatred) and racist actions (discrimination, bullying, social avoidance and scape-goating), so religionism on Hull's definition can generate similar intolerance in terms of beliefs, attitudes and actions. Just as racists may try to rationalize their beliefs and actions by providing arguments that they claim justify racial domination, so religionists may justify their prejudice and discrimination against other faiths in terms of their belief that their own religion is the only true one. And just as the institutional arrangements in a western country like the UK may reinforce the advantages already enjoyed by the white majority, so there is evidence of many institutional structures favouring Christianity and particularly the Church of England.

Personal prejudice and institutional discrimination are not the only kinds of racism, however, and other kinds may be linked more to religious pluralism than to religious exclusivism. 'Paternalistic racism' (Halstead, 1988, p. 151 ff.), for example, refers to the way that the freedom of Black and minority ethnic (BME) communities is defined and restricted by generally well-intentioned regulations that are drawn up by whites; it implies that whites have the right to interfere in the lives of BME communities for their own good and the power to define that good. It implies, perhaps in a rather subtle way, the superiority of those who set the agenda and may ultimately be little more than a more sophisticated form of social control (Husband and

Alam, 2011, p. 218). Once again, the parallel with religion is clear enough: the intention behind the development of a more pluralist religious education is benign, but the effect is to require a shift in the religious beliefs of many religious groups and thus to show disrespect to those believers and reinforce the superiority of those proposing the changes. The pluralist approach to religious education may thus not actually serve the purpose it is intended to, in terms of demonstrating respect and tolerance for diversity and contributing to community cohesion. The reason is that if children are being taught in school that their own faith is merely one of many equally valid faiths, they are being taught something very different from the more exclusivist message their own faith may proclaim (that their own faith is the true one). Effectively, a new faith is being taught in schools, one which highlights the importance of respect and tolerance for other religions in theory but does not extend this respect and tolerance in practice to the many believers who claim that their own faith is the true one. Ironically, the anti-religionist agenda for improving religious education may itself be religionist.

Religious truth, pluralism and metaphorical language

Given the fact that different faiths have massive doctrinal differences (as both authors agree), is it possible to talk of religious truth? Certainly many believers, whatever their particular faith, still appear to take it for granted that their own faith is not only true but 'comprehensive, incapable of abandonment and of central importance' (Griffiths, 2001, p. 12). So how should religious educators respond to the conflicting, yet totally sincere and deeply cherished, claims to truth of different faith groups? Should they follow the lead of the liberal state in refusing to side with any definitive version of religious truth for reasons set out earlier in this Afterword? Or should they act on the assumption that the different truth claims of different faiths are merely 'different manifestations of the Real to humanity … [which] do not contradict one another' (Hick, 2001, p. 169)? Davis, by arguing that faiths employing differing 'descriptions of a transcendent divinity may, despite this, be focusing on the same being', seems to support Hick's view. Barnes, on the other hand, argues that we should attempt to find ways of respecting different faiths that face up to, rather than gloss over, their differences of doctrine and practice. The concept of religious truth is a hugely complex one, and the most I can do in this section is to put up a few signposts on this rugged terrain.

The linguistic shift made in the previous paragraph, from 'truth' to 'truth claim', though common enough in secular and multi-faith contexts, begins to open up the problem. As Hardy (1982, p. 110) points out,

> Each religious tradition is, according to its nature, the vehicle for truth: and its truth is not dependent on the claims of its adherents that it is true *for* them – its truth does not rest on a truth claim, nor does it rely on the quality of arguments its adherents may advance for it. In fairness to its nature, and to its adherents, can it then be presented as a truth-*claim*, as truth *for* its adherents?

In other words, if you take what I call truth and call it merely a truth claim, then not only are you diminishing the value of what I hold dear and build my life upon, but you are also implying that the truths of my religious beliefs are dependent on how persuasive an argument I can make for them. But the common school, if it is to be fair to the different traditions and avoid indoctrination or proselytization, adopts a neutral position and treats them all with equal respect as 'truth claims'. In doing so, however, the sought-for neutrality is actually lost, because the question of their actual truth is prejudged by describing them as 'truth claims'. This distancing of any given tradition from the truth appears disrespectful to anyone committed to that tradition. So the crucial question is whether the diverse religious traditions of any given society can (to use Hardy's words again: 1982, p. 112) 'engage in real dialogue and mutual understanding without the initial supposition that each is less than the presentation of truth'. This is the point that Barnes is striving towards and what he means by real respect for diversity, the safeguarding of the truth in religious traditions. Davis, on the other hand, while avoiding claims that 'all religions are the same' (this volume, p. 109) or that 'everyone has their own route to the truth' (p. 64), argues that exclusive claims to truth, especially salvific exclusivism, are morally repulsive and that teaching 'in the pluralist spirit' (p. 112) should be a requirement both in common schools and in faith schools.

Exclusivism and pluralism are normally presented as two opposing approaches to the question of religious truth: exclusivists believe that religious truth is found only in the teachings of a single religion and that belonging to that religion is essential for salvation, while pluralists believe that truth may be found in different religions, all of which therefore deserve to be treated with equal respect in the public domain. Perhaps it is more helpful, however, to see these two as points on a continuum, with total exclusivism (the view that one religion has unique access to religious truth and no other religion possesses any religious truth) at one extreme and total pluralism (the view that all religions are on a par with regard to truth) at the other. In between are: moderate exclusivists who believe that some truths about God may be shared by other religions; inclusivists like Rahner who accept the absolute truth of one religion but also believe that followers of other religions can be saved through the one true religion; those like Cragg (1986) who are totally committed to the truth of their own tradition but nonetheless believe that they can accept insights from other religions; 'provisional pluralists' (Newbigin, 2001, p. 98) who argue that all religions should join forces to achieve a beneficent world order; and moderate pluralists like Cantwell Smith (1963) who argue that the central experience of God is the same for all believers in spite of the wide diversity of creeds, rituals, doctrines, values and community life.

It is not too difficult to locate Davis on this spectrum of positions: his complete rejection of exclusivism puts him on the pluralist side, but some distance from the extreme pluralism of John Hick because he does not talk of the equal worth and equal truth of all religions. Barnes is harder to locate on the spectrum, because he is not arguing in support of an exclusivist perspective, but in support of respect for exclusivism, as he takes religious diversity extremely seriously. Perhaps on this broad spectrum of positions, Barnes and Davis are not so far apart as they first appear. Each may in fact be arguing against a more extreme version of the position the other holds: Barnes may be right to argue that the liberal theological model with its emphasis on the equal truth of all religions does not show adequate respect for religious difference, but this is not exactly what Davis is claiming; and Davis may be right to argue that there is something arrogant, even unethical, about salvific exclusivism, but Barnes is not supporting such exclusivism either. We are now ready to turn back in conclusion to the implications of these arguments for religious education, but before we do so it is worth reflecting briefly on Davis's point about the inescapably metaphorical nature of religious language, because, among other things, it leads him to distinguish between 'literal truth' and 'profound truth'.

Davis is concerned to argue that apparently irreconcilable doctrinal differences between religions do not necessarily imply that either one or both faiths must be wrong; it may just be that the religions are using irreducibly metaphorical language which needs to be understood as such. An irreducible metaphor is one whose meaning can only be explained through other metaphors and which is not open to re-expression in literal terms. He uses the Muslim denial of the Christian doctrine that Jesus is the Son of God as a key example. The Muslim denial is based on the belief that God does not have a human form and therefore cannot literally have a son, but Davis believes that the problem largely disappears if Muslims come to understand that 'all Christians know that Jesus is not *literally* the Son of God' (this volume, p. 107). In case this sounds like a denial of a central Christian doctrine, he quickly explains that a 'denial of the literal truth is *not* the same as a denial of a profound truth' (p. 107). There are two problems with this argument, however. First, the recognition that the language is metaphorical does not necessarily put an end to serious disagreement over religious doctrine. For example, many Protestants believe that when Jesus took a loaf of bread at the Last Supper, said 'This is my body' and broke the bread, he was expressing in a visual metaphor or symbol what was soon going to happen to his own body; Catholics, on the other hand, believe that in some 'profound' sense the bread is actually transubstantiated into the body of Christ. Second, it is not clear exactly what is meant by 'a profound truth' here. A 'literal' truth presumably means a historical or scientific truth, one that can be verified in some way. But what is a 'profound' truth? To say that it means a spiritual truth or a truth which is not rationally verifiable does not get us very far; but to say that it is 'just a belief' seems to reduce its significance.

I want to suggest that in the context of religion the term 'truth' itself is being used metaphorically, and the point of the comparison implicit in the metaphor is certainty. The certainty that the believer may have about the truth of her beliefs is being implicitly compared to the certainty she feels about things that can be validated on an objective basis. The question where such spiritual certainty comes from, if it is not to be substantiated on objective rational grounds is open to a diversity of explanations. Wittgenstein (1958) suggests that there can be a sudden moment when such certainty comes to a person, though the ground will presumably have been already prepared by the processes of socialization. MacIntyre (1959) says that it is a matter of conversion, or spiritual experience. Others have seen its origin in the human will, or as a gift from God, or in a basic intuition about the existence of things. Whatever its origin within individuals, however, it is commitment to a publicly recognisable way of life of a community of believers that allows for a shared discourse of religious truth.

Liberalism, in insisting that religion is a matter of individual choice, misses or undervalues this notion of shared certainty and commitment, which Wittgenstein (1958, p. 226) calls a 'form of life' and Muslims call the *umma* (convictional community). The certainty is so deeply embedded in the consciousness of the community that very convincing grounds would have to be established for disrupting the community's structures by insisting that the beliefs must be subject to critical rational investigation and change; such grounds might include, for example, evidence that the beliefs are seriously damaging to the members of the community or to others. In the absence of such evidence, however, Wittgenstein argues that it is impossible to find criteria by which to judge that the religious views of one community are inferior to those of another. One is simply committed to them or not, and it is impossible to justify (or condemn) such a commitment outside the way of life of which it forms a part. This provides a strong case for the need to respect diverse religious traditions and the 'profound truths' on which they are based, rather than seeking to transform these into something closer to one's own beliefs in the name of equality.

Tolerance, respect and religious education

We can now return to Barnes' central argument that recent religious education in England has largely failed in its attempt to prepare children for life in a multicultural society by adopting a neutral approach based on the view that the different religions have much in common and are essentially in agreement. Children are encouraged to enter imaginatively into the experiences of different faiths and develop empathy and acceptance but the approach avoids the discussion of doctrinal differences. Religious education fails to respect the distinctive truth claims of each individual religion and effectively, by teaching the equal worth and implying the equal truth of all religions, teaches a different religion itself (which it is clearly not the role of religious education to do). Pluralist or multi-faith religious education is thus incapable of challenging intolerance and developing respect for diversity because it does not take difference seriously enough. It misrepresents religious beliefs and therefore does not itself demonstrate the respect it teaches. Religious education, Barnes argues, must abandon theological models that base respect for others on the claim that the different religions are in essential agreement and of equal validity and must teach respect for persons as a value in its own right irrespective of their religious beliefs and commitments.

Ironically perhaps (since he rejects what he calls the 'liberal model' of religious education, i.e. the pluralist or multi-faith approach), Barnes appears closer to the secular liberal framework of values discussed earlier than Davis, because he does not want to side with any particular religious worldview (unlike Davis who rejects exclusivist worldviews). He also takes tolerance and respect for persons as primary values. For him, respect for the beliefs of others is a secondary value, derived from respect for persons, and he argues strongly that it is possible to respect a person *and* to respect their right to hold their own beliefs and values (based on the liberal value of freedom of conviction) without agreeing in any way with those beliefs. This is precisely what tolerance is: 'a deliberate choice not to interfere with conduct of which one disapproves' (Horton, 1993,

p. 3). Barnes therefore argues that religious education should not base its teaching of respect for others on the assumption that all religions involve some kind of common quest. Instead, it should aim to encourage students to engage fully and critically with the claims and commitments of different religions, acknowledge the differences without disguising them or implying some underlying unity and make their own free choices while recognizing the unacceptability of religious intolerance and the importance of recognizing the rights of others to believe something different from oneself.

In reply, Davis's defence of a 'modest' form of religious pluralism depends on two main arguments. First, he claims that that pluralist religious education does not misrepresent different world faiths, because the different faiths may be focusing on the same transcendental being in spite of their differences of belief and practice, and in any case the metaphorical nature of religious language helps us to understand how differences of interpretation may arise. Second, and more briefly, he argues that it is 'extraordinarily difficult' to respect a person if one is certain their beliefs are untrue. This runs counter to liberalism, which bases respect for persons on their unique status as moral agents and nothing else, but for Davis it is very hard in practice to separate this minimal conception of personhood from one's broader judgement about the truth or otherwise of their beliefs and values. In any case, he argues, exclusivist beliefs may make people arrogant and insensitive to others and may make intolerance and conflict more likely.

At the heart of the debate therefore is the question whether we can separate out our moral duty of respect for persons with whom we disagree from our rejection of their beliefs and values, as liberalism suggests, or whether the actual disagreement is likely to have an adverse effect on our respect. For Peterson et al. (1991, p. 221), there is no question that evaluating persons' truth claims and relating to them as persons are entirely separate, one being an epistemological matter and the other a moral one:

> ... we should not make the faulty inference that statements regarding how we should treat those with whom we disagree follow directly from epistemological claims about the truths or falsehoods they hold. That people hold a false belief does not

allow us to mistreat them, nor should we give them special treatment if they make true claims.

On Barnes' view it is not conviction of the rightness of one's beliefs that is the problem, but intolerance of others holding different beliefs. Rather than seeking to change their convictions (from exclusivist to pluralist) therefore, we should put more emphasis on changing the attitude of individuals towards other persons and their beliefs (from intolerance to tolerance). But Hull says that tolerance is not enough (2000, p. 82) and (as already noted) argues for a comprehensive programme of 'anti-religionist' education. To the extent that he believes religious education should teach children the 'compelling reasons for pluralism' and 'how damaging and destructive religious exclusivism can be' (this volume, p. 63) Davis appears to agree with him.

The problem with Hull's approach, however, as we have seen, is the way 'religionism' is conceived. Religionism seems to be understood as a specific form of cultural racism, which I have defined elsewhere as a form of domination and oppression that 'demands cultural conformity where it is neither necessary nor perhaps even desirable, and penalizes people unjustly for failure to conform' (Halstead, 1988, p. 146). If Hull takes for granted the superiority of religious pluralism and focuses largely or exclusively on shared beliefs and inter-faith topics in Religious Education, it is likely that the beliefs and practices of exclusivist faiths will be undervalued and the self-awareness of believers harmed. Such an attitude towards exclusivists demonstrates a lack of respect by paying inadequate attention to the distinctive needs, experiences and wishes of minority faiths. There are certainly groups for whom the message that all religions are equally valid and therefore deserve equal attention in Religious Education would go against the grain of their commitments and identity.

Muslims in England, for example, may wish to ask a number of searching questions. Does the teaching about Islam that is integrated into religious education in English state schools actually provide young people with accurate knowledge about Islam, or does it give a false impression of cultural conformity across the Muslim world and present the faith through a template (such as an emphasis in primary religious education on the use of religious artefacts) which does not help them to develop a clear understanding of Islam? Does the teaching contribute to inter-cultural understanding, encourage positive, respectful attitudes to Muslims and help to free non-Muslim young people from inherited biases and cultural insensitivity, or does it draw attention to the alien nature of some Islamic religious and cultural practices and reinforce prejudice and stereotyping? Does it support the developing identity of Muslim children in England or does it destabilize them by implying that their faith is just one of a number of equally valid religions between which they are free to make their own choices? It seems unlikely that the five hours or so per year spent studying Islam as part of religious education is enough to achieve any positive goals – at least, unless it is supplemented with (a) positive references to Islam and the Muslim contribution to learning and culture across many other subjects of the National Curriculum and (b) a Muslim-friendly approach to other aspects of school life, which will carry important hidden-curriculum messages about respect for Muslims and their faith and help to shape non-Muslim students' attitudes in a positive way.

Concluding remarks

In the much celebrated novel *Knowledge of Angels* (Paton Walsh, 1994), the arrival of an exhausted swimmer on the shores of Grandinsula brings the first experience of genuine diversity to the pre-Reformation Christian island. The swimmer is Palinor, a prince from a distant country called Aclar where those of all faiths or none enjoy equal respect. Palinor becomes a spokesman for liberal humanist values in the novel, but as an avowed atheist he should under the island's laws be put to death as a heretic. The well-meaning Severo, cardinal and prince of the island, tries to find a way of saving him from this fate, but the saintly Beneditx who is given the task of converting him, ends up losing his own faith. With the arrival of Fra Murta, the sinister and unyielding Inquisitor from Rome, however, the story moves to a gruesome climax, both for Palinor and perhaps ultimately for the whole island.

The story provides space for philosophical and theological debate about many of the main themes that have been discussed in the present volume, including freedom, diversity, tolerance, compromise, religious certainty and the way religious exclusivity can spawn intolerance and violence. It also adds significant insights to our own discussions. First, it highlights the complexity of the concept of respect for persons and stresses the need to see others as fully human, not just as the bearers of certain religious doctrines or certain attitudes to other faiths. Second, the story shows that there can be many different shades of religious exclusivism, from benign to lethal, and it is unhelpful to create stereotypes by tarring them all with the same brush; we need a more nuanced approach to exclusivist and fundamentalist faiths rather than the blanket condemnations provided by some philosophers. Third, the gulf that exists between the beliefs of different individuals or groups (as between liberals and fundamentalists in the story) is often deep-rooted and (as Barnes suggests) cannot be ignored.

Earlier in the Afterword it was implied that there might be problems in tying religious education too closely to liberal education, both because the underlying values of religion and liberalism are very different and because the distinctive voice of religion (in terms of the social gospel, for example, and the principle of service to others) might be lost in the rights-talk of liberalism. For some, it is the role of religious education to spearhead a critical response to liberal values. Even more importantly, there is a danger that what Taylor (1992) calls the 'politics of equal recognition' may lead to an undermining of an individual's or group's distinctive identity and commitments, because it involves treating people the same on the basis of their common humanity and 'equal dignity' rather than acknowledging deep-seated differences. All too often this leads to the expectation that minority groups will assimilate. Taylor contrasts this with what he calls the 'politics of difference', which recognizes the unique identity of individuals and groups: 'it is precisely this distinctness that has been ignored, glossed over, assimilated to a dominant or majority identity' (Taylor, 1992, p. 38). Husband and Alam (2011, p. 223) similarly argue that we must '*define our collective identity through the way we live with difference, rather than by the desperate assertion of sameness*'. What Barnes has successfully achieved in his essay is to apply this political thinking to the specific issue of religious education and to demonstrate the damagingly homogenizing effect of pluralist approaches.

Nevertheless, religious education and liberal education do share some common purposes, including the promotion of respect for persons and the development of critical rationality, and many people will support a collaborative approach in these areas. Respect for persons is a key religious concept, as well as a moral and philosophical one (Downie and Telfer, 1969). Religious education can provide not only knowledge and understanding of the distinctive teachings of different religions but also a sense of how the essential humanity of believers comes across in their everyday lives and values. If ignorance is one of the main causes of prejudice, fear and suspicion, religious education can help to break down stereotypes of believers and misconceptions of their beliefs. Certainly it may be easier to respect people you know something about. At the same time, religious education can help children to reflect critically on the different teachings and values that different religions hold as true. Even exclusivists may recognize that there is political and social benefit in studying different religions so that people can live together in harmony and cohesion, showing respect to those different from ourselves and avoiding giving offence. Some may recognize the possibility of enriching their own lives in the process.

Further Reading

Adler, M. J. (1990), *Truth in Religion: The Plurality of Religions and the Unity of Truth*, New York: Macmillan.

Alston, W. (1989), *Divine Nature and Human Language*, Ithaca: Cornell University Press.

Barnes, L. P. (2014a), *Education, Religion and Diversity: Developing a New Model of Religious Education*, London: Routledge.

———. (2014b), 'The Demise and Rebirth of Moral Education in English Religious Education', in M. Felderhof and P. Thompson (eds), *Teaching Virtue: The Contribution of Religious Education*, London: Bloomsbury.

Bates, D., Durka, G. and Schweitzer, F. (eds) (2006), *Education, Religion and Society: Essays in Honour of John M. Hull*, Abingdon: Routledge.

Felderhof, M. Thompson, P. and Torevell, D. (eds) (2007), *Inspiring Faith in Schools: Studies in Religious Education*, Aldershot: Ashgate.

Griffiths, P. J. (2001), *Problems of Religious Diversity*, Oxford: Blackwell.

Hick, J. (2005), *The Metaphor of God Incarnate*, London: SCM Press.

Hick, J. and Knitter, P. (eds) (2005), *The Myth of Christian Uniqueness: Towards a Pluralist Theology of Religion*, Eugene: Wipf and Stock.

Jackson, R. (1997), *Religious Education: An Interpretive Approach*, London: Hodder and Stoughton.

———. (2004), *Rethinking Religious Education and Plurality: Issues in Diversity and Pedagogy*, London: RoutledgeFalmer.

Nord, W. A. (2010), *Does God Make a Difference? Teaching Religion Seriously in Our Schools and Universities*, New York: Oxford University Press.

Bibliography

Allen, C. (2010), *Islamophobia*, London: Ashgate.

Alston, W. (1964), *Philosophy of Language*, Englewood Cliffs: Prentice Hall.

———. (1995), 'Realism and the Christian Faith', *International Journal for Philosophy of Religion*, 38: 37–60.

———. (2005), 'Religious Language', in W. Wainwright (ed.), *The Oxford Handbook of Philosophy of Religion*, Oxford: Oxford University Press, pp. 220–224.

Anderson, J. (2005), 'In Defence of Mystery: A Reply to Dale Tuggy', *Religious Studies*, 41(2): 145–163.

Aquinas, T. (1964), *Summa Theologiae*, in Herbert McCabe (trans.), London: Eyre and Spottiswoode.

Augustine (1972), *City of God*, Harmondsworth: Penguin Books.

Barnes, L. P. (2014a), *Education, Religion and Diversity: Developing a New Model of Religious Education*, London: Routledge.

———. (2014b), 'The Demise and Rebirth of Moral Education in English Religious Education', in M. Felderhof and P. Thompson (eds), *Teaching Virtue: The Contribution of Religious Education*, London: Bloomsbury, pp. 54–70.

Barnes, L. P. and Felderhof, M. (2014), 'Reviewing the Religious Education Review', *Journal of Beliefs and Values*, 35(1): 108–117.

Basinger, D. (1991), 'Divine Omniscience and the Soteriological Problem of Evil: Is the Type of Knowledge God Possesses Relevant?', *Religious Studies*, 28: 1–18.

Bates, D. (1996), 'Christianity, Culture and Other Religions (Part 2): F H Hilliard, Ninian Smart and the 1988 Education Reform Act', *British Journal of Religious Education*, 18(2): 85–102.

Black, M. (1979), 'More about Metaphor', in A. Ortony (ed.), *Metaphor and Thought*, Cambridge: Cambridge University Press, pp. 19–43.

Boër, S. E. and Lycan, W. G. (1975), 'Knowing Who', *Philosophical Studies*, 28: 299–344.

Braithwaite, Richard (1970), 'An Empiricist's View of the Nature of Religious Belief', in Basil Mitchell (ed.). *The Philosophy of Religion*, Oxford: Oxford University Press, pp. 72–91.

Byrne, P. (1982), 'John Hick's Philosophy of World Religions', *Scottish Journal of Theology*, 35: 289–301.

Calvin, J. (1960), *Institutes of the Christian Religion*, in J. McNeill, (ed.), Ford Lewis Battles (trans.), 2 vols., Philadelphia: Westminster Press. 3.23.2, pp. 949–950.

Cantwell Smith, W. (1963), *The Meaning and End of Religion*, New York: Macmillan.

———. (2001), 'The Christian in a Religiously Plural World', in J. Hick and B. Hebblethwaite (eds), *Christianity and Other Religions: Selected Readings*, Oxford: Oneworld, pp. 44–58.

Carter, I. (2013), 'Are Toleration and Respect Compatible?', *Journal of Applied Philosophy*, 30(3): 195–208.

Copley, T. (2008), *Teaching Religion: Sixty Years of Religious Education in England and Wales*, Exeter: University of Exeter Press.

Cragg, K. (1986), *The Christ and the Faiths*, London: SPCK.

Darwall, S. (1977). 'Two Kinds of Respect', *Ethics*, 88(1): 36–49.

Davidson, D. (1980), 'What Metaphors Mean', in M. Platts (ed.), *Reference, Truth and Reality*, London: Routledge & Kegan Paul, pp. 238–254.

———. (2001), 'Subjective, Intersubjective, Objective', *Philosophical Essays Volume 3*, Oxford: Clarendon Press.

Department for Children, Schools and Families (2007), *Guidance on the Duty to Promote Community Cohesion*, Nottingham: DCSF.

Donnellan, K. (1966), 'Reference and Definite Descriptions', *The Philosophical Review*, 77: 281–304.

Downie, R. S. and Telfer, E. (1969), *Respect for Persons*, London: George Allen & Unwin.

Esposito, J. L. and Kalin, I. (eds) (2011), *Islamophobia: the Challenge of Pluralism in the 21st Century*, New York: Oxford University Press.

Geach, P. (1994), 'The Moral Law and the Law of God', in J. Graf Haber (ed.), *Absolutism and Its Consequentialist Critics*, Maryland: Rowman & Littlefield, pp. 63–72.

Geertz, C. (1985), 'Religion as a Cultural System', in M. Banton (ed.), *Anthropological Approaches to the Study of Religion*, London: Tavistock Publishers, pp. 1–46.

Griffiths, P. J. (2001), *Problems of Religious Diversity*, Oxford: Blackwell.

Grimmitt, M. (1973/1978, 2nd edition), *What Can I Do in RE?*, Great Wakering: Mayhew-McCrimmon.

———. (1987), *Religious Education and Human Development*, Essex, Great Wakering: McCrimmons.

Halstead, J. M. (1988), *Education, Justice and Cultural Diversity*, London: Falmer Press.

———. (2005), 'British Muslims and Education', in T. Choudhury (ed.) *Muslims in the UK: Policies for Engaged Citizens*, Budapest: Open Society Institute, pp. 101–191.

———. (2010), 'In Defense of Multiculturalism', in Y. Raley and G. Preyer (eds), *Philosophy of Education in the Era of Globalization*, New York: Routledge, pp. 181–197.

Hardy, D. W. (1982), 'Truth in Religious Education: Further Reflections on the Implications of Pluralism', in J. M. Hull (ed.), *New Directions in Religious Education*, Lewes: Falmer Press, pp. 109–118.

Hay, D. (1977), 'Religious Experience and Education', *Learning for Living*, 16(4): 156–161.

Hick, J. (1977), 'Jesus and the World Religions', in J. Hick (ed.), *The Myth of God Incarnate*, London: SCM Press, pp. 167–185.

———. (2001), 'The Theological Challenge of Religious Pluralism', in J. Hick and B. Hebblethwaite (eds), *Christianity and Other Religions: Selected Readings*, Oxford: Oneworld, pp. 156–171.

———. (2004), *An Interpretation of Religion: Human Responses to the Transcendent*, 2nd e New Haven: Yale University Press (1989).

Horton, J. (ed.) (1993), *Liberalism, Multiculturalism and Toleration*, London: Macmillan.

Hull, J. M. (1982), *New Directions in Religious Education*, Lewes: Falmer Press.

———. (1992), 'The Transmission of Religious Prejudice', *British Journal of Religious Education*, 14(2): 69–72.

———. (2000), 'Religionism and Religious Education', in M. Leicester, C. Modgil and S. Modgil (eds), *Education, Culture and Values: Spiritual and Religious Education, Volume 5*, London: Falmer Press, pp. 75–85.

Husband, C. and Alam, Y. (2011), *Social Cohesion and Counter-Terrorism: a Policy Contraction?* Bristol: Policy Press.

Jackson, F. (1977), *Perception*, Cambridge: Cambridge University Press, Chapter 1.

Jackson, R. (1997), *Religious Education: An Interpretive Approach*, London: Hodder and Stoughton.

———. (2004), *Rethinking Religious Education and Plurality: Issues in Diversity and Pedagogy*, London: RoutledgeFalmer.

Johnston, C. (1996), *Christian Teachers and World Faiths*, Derby: Christian Education Movement.

Kay, W. K. (1997), 'Phenomenology, Religious Education, and Piaget', *Religion*, 27(3): 275–283.

Kay, W. K. and Smith, D. L. (2000), 'Religious Terms and Attitudes in the Classroom' (Part 1), *British Journal of Religious Education*, 22(2): 81–90.

Lindbeck, G. A. (1984), *The Nature of Doctrine: Religion and Theology in a Postliberal Age*, London: SPCK.

Macedo, S. (2000), *Diversity and Distrust: Civic Education in a Multicultural Democracy*, Cambridge: Harvard University Press.

MacIntyre, A. (1959), *Metaphysical Belief*, New York: Ithaca.

Marty, M. E. (2011), 'Historical Reflections on Religious Diversity', in C. Meister (ed.), *The Oxford Handbook of Religious Diversity*, Oxford: Oxford University Press.

Marvell, J. (1976), 'Phenomenology and the Future of Religious Education', *Learning for Living*, 16(1): 4–8.

———. (1982), 'Phenomenology and the Future of Religious Education', in J. Hull (ed.), *New Directions in Religious Education*, Lewes: Falmer Press.

McDowell, J. (1980), 'On the Sense and Reference of a Proper Name', in M. Platts (ed.), *Reference, Truth and Reality*, London: Routledge and Kegan Paul.

McLaughlin, T. H. (1984), 'Parental Rights and the Religious Upbringing of Children', *Journal of Philosophy of Education*, 18(1): 75–83.

Miller, J. (2009), 'So, What Do the Toledo Guiding Principles Have to Do With Me?' *Resource*, 31(2): 6–9.

Minney, R. (1975), *Of Many Mouths and Eyes*, London: Hodder and Stoughton.

Newbigin, L. (2001), 'Teaching Religion in a Secular Plural Society', in J. M. Hull (ed.), *New Directions in Religious Education*, Lewes: Falmer Press, pp. 97–107.

Office for National Statistics (ONS) (2013), *What Does the Census Tell Us about Religion in 2011?* www.ons.gov.uk/home [accessed 2 June 2014].

Olscamp, P. (1970), 'How Some Metaphors May Be True or False', *The Journal of Aesthetics and Art Criticism*, 29(1): 77–86.

Otto, R. (1958), *The Idea of the Holy: An Inquiry into the Non-Rational Factor in the Idea of the Divine and Its Relation to the Rational*, 2nd edition, in John W. Harvey (trans.), Oxford: Oxford University Press.

Parker-Jenkins, M., Glenn, M. and Janmaat, J. G. (2014), *Reaching In, Reaching Out: Faith Schools, Community Engagement and 21st-Century Skills for Intercultural Understanding*, London: Institute of Education Press.

Paton Walsh, J. (1994), *Knowledge of Angels*, Cambridge: Colt Books.

Peterson, M., Hasker, W., Reichenbach, B. and Basinger, D. (1991), *Reason and Religious Belief: An Introduction to the Philosophy of Religion*, New York: Oxford University Press.

Qualifications and Curriculum Authority (2004), *Non-Statutory National Framework for Religious Education*, London: QCA.

Radford, M. (1999), 'Religious Education, Spiritual Experience and Truth', *British Journal of Religious Education*, 21(3): 166–174.

Rawls, J. (1993), *Political Liberalism*, New York: Columbia University Press.

Raz, J. (2001), *Value, Respect and Attachment*, Cambridge: Cambridge University Press.

Religious Education Council of England and Wales (2013), *A Review of Religious Education in England*, RE Council.

Roebben, B. (2007), 'School, Religion and Diversity: A West-European Perspective on Religious Identity Formation', *Journal of Religious Education*, 55(3): 39–45.

Ruhmkorff, S. (2013), 'The Incompatibility Problem and Religious Pluralism Beyond Hick', *Philosophy Compass*, 8(5): 510–522.

Schleiermacher, F. ([1830]1928), *The Christian Faith*, Edinburgh: T & T Clark.

———. ([1799]1958), *On Religion: Speeches to Its Cultural Despisers*, New York: Harper & Row.

Schools Council (1971), *Working Paper 36: Religious Education in Secondary Schools*, London: Evans/Methuen.

Searle, J. (1969), *Speech Acts: An Essay in the Philosophy of Language*. Cambridge: Cambridge University Press.

———. (1979), 'Metaphor', in A. Ortony (ed.), *Metaphor and Thought*, Cambridge: Cambridge University Press.

Smith, D. L. and Kay, W. K. (2000), 'Religious Terms and Attitudes in the Classroom' (Part 2), *British Journal of Religious Education*, 22(2): 181–191.

Sosa, E. (1970), 'Propositional Attitudes de Dictu and de Re', *The Journal of Philosophy*, 67(21): 883–896.

Stark, R. (2013), *America's Blessings: How Religion Benefits Everyone, Including Atheists*, West Conshohocken: Templeton Foundation Press.

Street, R. (2007), *Religious Education in Anglican Voluntary Aided Secondary Schools: Moving from Transmission to Transformation*, unpublished Ph.D. thesis, King's College London.

Tanner, K. (2013), 'Creation ex nihilo as Mixed Metaphor', *Modern Theology*, 29(2): 138–155.

Taylor, C. (1992), *Multiculturalism and 'the Politics of Recognition'*, Princeton: Princeton University Press.

Tuggy, D. (2003), 'The Unfinished Business of Trinitarian Theorizing', *Religious Studies*, 39(2): 165–183.

Wittgenstein, L. (1958), *Philosophical Investigations*, Oxford: Blackwell.

Wright, A. (2004), *Religion, Education and Post Modernity*, London: RoutledgeFalmer.

Index

WITHDRAWAL